UNITS IN ENGLISH

Literacy Standards
for NCEA Level 1

Angela Finestone

PEARSON
Longman

Acknowledgements

I would like to thank all the people who have encouraged and supported me throughout the development of this text.

I would like to express my gratitude to the students I have worked with over the past years. This experience has inspired me to explore and develop resources to help make achievement in NCEA a reality.

The following people have encouraged me, both personally and professionally: Heather Condie, Paul Green, Pat Ramiah and Janine Rayner and, of course, my parents and my eternally patient husband Nick.

Angela Finestone

www.pearsoned.co.nz

Your comments on this book are welcome at
feedback@pearsoned.co.nz

Pearson Education New Zealand
a division of Pearson New Zealand Ltd
67 Apollo Drive, Rosedale, North Shore 0632, New Zealand

Associated companies throughout the world

© Pearson Education New Zealand 2008

ISBN: 978-1-4425-0187-4

Produced by Pearson Education New Zealand

Commissioning Editor: Bronwen Nicholson
Editor: Sue Hall
Designer: Thinkspace Design/Esther Chua
Page layout: Thinkspace Design/Esther Chua
Cover: Marie Low
Cover photos: © Jose Antonio Sánchez Reyes/Dreamstime.com,
© Alex Brosa/Dreamstime.com, © Dreamstime Agency/Dreamstime.com

Printed in Malaysia (CTP-VP)
Typeset in ITC Novarese 10.5/12pt

We use **paper from sustainable forestry**

Contents

Colour section: static images, Visuals I–IV

Introduction

I am passionate about teaching English and I strongly believe that NCEA has brought in a change for the better; especially for you as students. This NCEA Level 1 English course has been designed to make achievement a reality for you. I have found that each of the units covered is user-friendly and carefully guides you as you learn. I have offered these unit standards to my own classes since NCEA began and my students have achieved many successes. Some have even surprised themselves with their own results.

I believe that achieving NCEA Level One is within the reach of all Year 11 and 12 students. The units explored in this text all relate to 'real life' issues and most of them work on developing practical literacy skills you will find useful in other subjects and in your future learning and working.

Whether you use a handful of the units in this text or all of them, I hope that working with this text will help you to achieve your own success in NCEA.

NCEA English Level 1: a unit standards course

	Unit standard course outline	Credits
10792	Write formal personal correspondence.	3
2977	Read texts for practical purposes.	4
8808	Read an inclusive range of written texts and record the reading experience.	3
8810	Read an inclusive range of visual texts and record the reading experience.	2
8811	Collect information using a range of oral, written, and visual sources and methods.	3
8812	Produce transactional written text in simple forms.	4
8813	Produce poetic written text in simple forms.	4
8814	Write regular responses to texts and reflect on personal learning.	2
8817	Listen attentively during and interact in discussion.	2
12411	Explore language and think critically about transactional written text.	3
12417	Present a static image using verbal and visual features.	2

To achieve NCEA Level 1 you must earn a total of 80 credits across a range of subjects. These must include:

- eight numeracy credits (from your Maths programme)
- eight literacy credits (from your English programme).

UNIT 1 Writing formal personal correspondence

Unit Standard 10792: what is it all about?

For this unit standard you will need to write three letters. At least one of these should be a traditional letter and another should be an email letter.

In this unit we will be writing two traditional post letters and one email letter.

Working out what we already know

Our brains are like filing cabinets or folders in software – any time we experience or learn something new, it's filed.

By brainstorming we can activate (set in motion) the information we already know about a topic. This means that when we learn new things we can add to the file which already exists.

How do we brainstorm?

One way of brainstorming is to write the name of your topic in the middle of a page and write down any ideas you have around it. For example, to begin a brainstorm on letter writing, you would write the topic 'Letter writing' in the middle of your page. Starter ideas you might use are:

- We write letters because …
- A letter normally has …
- Correspondence means …

How will I be assessed?

This unit standard is worth three credits.
We will be writing three letters for this unit standard:

- one letter of request
- one letter of complaint
- one email letter.

Your first two letters are traditional post letters and will be assessed by the following elements and performance criteria. You need to meet all performance criteria for each of your three letters to earn your three credits.

Your third letter will be an email letter and this will be assessed by the email marking criteria on page 10.

Writing
Elements and performance criteria for Unit Standard 10792
Write formal personal correspondence.

Element 1
Write formal personal correspondence by traditional post (a letter).

Performance criteria

1.1   The letter is addressed to the intended person, and the purpose of the letter is stated at or near the beginning.

1.2   The information presented is accurate, clear, relevant, and ordered in a sequence which fits the context.

1.3   Information is presented so that the content, vocabulary, and tone fit the context, subject matter, and audience.

1.4   Punctuation is accurate in terms of full stops, capital letters, and commas.

1.5   Spelling is accurate at least 90% of the time.

1.6   A formal letter format is followed, and the form of address used fits the context and the relationship between writer and receiver.

  Task: Now, complete the self-analysis test your teacher gives you.

Starter activities

 Task: The following words are frequently used in letter writing, so they are words you need to know. Read the three words on each line and, in your English book, write down the one you think has been spelt correctly.

	A	B	C
1	somethink	something	somthing
2	a lot	alot	alott
3	favorite	favurite	favourite
4	esential	essentail	essential
5	diffrent	different	diferent
6	believe	beleive	believ
7	probably	probly	probley
8	apreciate	apprecate	appreciate
9	proffesional	professional	profesional
10	aplication	applicaton	application
11	luckely	luckly	luckily
12	differcult	difficult	dificult
13	commitment	committment	comittment
14	doesn't	does'nt	dosn't
15	approprate	apropriate	appropriate
16	intrested	interested	interrested
17	recognise	reconise	recgonise
18	personal qualites	personal qualities	personel qualities
19	responsible	responsibel	responsable
20	mannager	manerger	manager

Task: Find a formal alternative for these slang sentences. The first one has already been done for you.

1 See ya   *I hope to hear from you soon.*
2 Call me asap.
3 Get back to me when you can.
4 The product you sold me sucks.

The letter writing process

Each time you draft a letter you need to follow the letter writing process.

Step 1

Decide on your topic and brainstorm your ideas.

- Write the name of your topic in the middle of the page and write down all your ideas around it.
- Have a close look at the ideas you have written down. Underline your most important ideas.
- Your teacher will give you a letter writing format, copy out this format.
- Draw up the following chart in your English book. Use the ideas from your first brainstorm to complete the chart.

Letter number	Beginning paragraph	Middle paragraph	Last paragraph
Purpose:			
Main idea:			
Supporting ideas:			

Step 2

Write your draft. Make sure you are aware of your audience and purpose.
Audience: How do I know who my audience is?

- Your audience is the person (or people) who will be reading your letter.

Purpose: How do I know what my purpose is?

- Your purpose is the reason you are writing the letter. There are many purposes or reasons to write a letter. Your purpose could be to inform or to persuade or even to complain.

Step 3

Re-read your draft. In a quiet voice, read your letter aloud. Check that each sentence makes sense. Then check the spelling of any words you are unsure about.
Ask yourself:

- Am I getting my purpose across?
- Do all my sentences make sense?
- Is my language appropriate?
- Have I used specific details where necessary?

Step 4

Peer proofread. Get another classmate to proofread your work to make sure it makes sense. While they proofread your letter, proofread theirs.

   Afterwards, sign your classmate's work (to show that you've proofread it) and make two comments:

1   One thing you did well was …
2   One thing you could improve on is …

Step 5

Have another look at your letter. Rewrite your draft and make sure you include any corrections or changes that need to be made.

Step 6

Hand in your second draft letter to your teacher.

 Note: Your teacher will provide you with a letter writing format. Look at this closely, because this is how you set out a letter.

Getting ready to write

Before you start writing any letters you need to be aware of these three things.

- **Purpose:** Why am I writing a letter? What do I want to achieve by communicating with this person/organisation?
- **Audience:** Who will be reading my letter? Why am I writing to this particular person?
- **Topic:** What is my letter about? What points do I need to make?

Purpose

The purpose is the reason for something – why we are doing it. Before we write a letter we need to be aware of the purpose.

What are some common purposes for writing letters?

- to apply for a job
- to thank someone
- to complain about something
- to request information
- to provide someone with information

Audience

When we write formal personal letters it is important to keep our language formal. Formal language is universal – it follows certain rules and standards. By using formal writing we can make sure that our message is clear and easily understood.

Task: Look closely at the box of words below. Write up the headings Formal language and Casual language in your English book and then list the following words under the appropriate heading.

yes	items	stuff	okay
appropriate	How's it?	best wishes	G'day
sux	yeah	my mates	Dear Sir/Madam
Yours sincerely	professional	stingy	suitable

Tone

Tone is the feeling or mood of something.

When we write letters it's important to keep a formal tone. This means that you must use formal language and be polite at all times, even if you're writing a complaint letter.

If you're really angry about something which has happened, you may feel like using offensive language – but this is not appropriate. Consider the person who will be reading your letter. They're more likely to read your side of the story and take action if you're polite and respectful.

Task: Look at the following two paragraphs. Both writers complain about the same issue but the tone is very different. Read them both carefully and decide which letter is more appropriate.

Paragraph A
I'm pissed off about the way we were treated at your restaurant when we went on Saturday. The stupid waitress sucked and she should've been nicer to us …

Paragraph B
I am very upset about the service I received at your restaurant on Saturday 7 June. My family and I found your waitress Laura was unprofessional …

If you were the owner of this restaurant, which letter would you choose to answer?

Applying for a job: personal qualities

When applying for a job you need to 'put your best foot forward'! This means that you need to 'sell yourself' and let your potential employer know that you're right for the job. One way you can do this is by writing about some of your personal qualities. The table below shows some personal qualities that prospective employers are often looking for.

honesty	commitment	responsibility	motivation
patience	reliability	enthusiasm	trustworthiness
co-operation	persistence	punctuality	energy

Task: Match the following personal qualities with their correct definitions. Write the numbers and corresponding letters in your English book. You may need to use a dictionary to assist you.

	Personal quality		Definition
1	honesty	a	An obligation or undertaking to do something.
2	patience	b	A strong interest or admiration for something.
3	co-operation	c	To endure, persist or to keep going.
4	commitment	d	To have a motive or purpose which drives you.
5	reliability	e	To be on time, not to be early or late.
6	persistence	f	To be deserving of trust.
7	responsibility	g	To be trusted or relied upon.
8	enthusiasm	h	To be able to act independently and to make decisions.
9	punctuality	i	To not cheat or steal, to be truthful.
10	motivation	j	To be active and fit.
11	trustworthiness	k	To be calm and tolerant when dealing with difficult situations.
12	energy	l	To work with others to achieve a common goal.

What other qualities can you think of?

Useful tip

If you're writing to someone from the same city as you, you don't need to add the city under the suburb. However, if the person you're writing to lives in a different city from you, make sure you record your city (after your address details) and their city (after their address details).

Task: Your teacher will give you a letter of request. Read this carefully, identify and correct the errors.

Writing your letter of request

Your purpose: is to apply for a job **or** to request information about a topic.
Your audience: the person who is advertising the job or someone who has information about a topic which interests you.
Your topic: the topic you are requesting information about
        – a job application **or** a request for information.

Use one of the following formats as a guide.

Format: request letter – job application

Paragraph 1	Your first sentence must let the reader know why you are writing.
I am responding to the job vacancy you advertised in …	
	Explain where you found the job vacancy and identify the job you're applying for. (Companies often advertise more than one job at once).
I am interested in this job / position because …	
	Express your interest in the job.
Paragraph 2	Introduce yourself.
I am a student at …	
	Explain why you would be suitable for the job. 'Sell yourself' by writing about your personal qualities.
I believe I would be suitable for this job because … *I am …*	
	For a part time job, make sure you mention your availability for work.
I am available on … from …	
Paragraph 3	Sum up your letter by thanking your reader.
I appreciate this opportunity to …	
	Provide your phone number and/or email address (optional). End on a positive note, which suggests that you are expecting a reply.
I look forward to …	

Format: request letter – requesting information

Paragraph 1	Your first sentence must let the reader know why you are writing.
I would like to request some information about … *I would like to request …*	
	Explain why you are writing. To request some information about a topic you're researching, e.g. your family genealogy.
I am interested in this topic because …	
Paragraph 2	Introduce yourself. Briefly explain who you are.
I am a student at …	
	Explain why you want this information. How would it be useful for you? Be specific about the information you are after. For example, if you are researching the topic of Cycling, narrow it down to one area; 'New Zealand cycling trends in the 1990s'.
Paragraph 3	Sum up your letter by thanking your reader.
I would appreciate it if you could …	
	Provide your phone number and/or email address (optional). End with a positive note, which suggests that you are expecting a reply.
I look forward to …	

Writing your letter of complaint

Your purpose: to complain about something
Your audience: the person you're complaining to. e.g. a restaurant manager
Your topic: The problem, incident or situation you are complaining about:
- receiving bad service **or**
- a faulty product.

 Note: Before you begin your own letter, your teacher will provide you with an exemplar, an example of a letter of complaint which has passed the marking criteria for this unit.

To complain about bad service

 Task: Brainstorm all the things that could go wrong in a visit to a restaurant. Then come up with some language which you can use to explain these problems. The following table is an example of how to draw up your brainstormed ideas.

Brainstormed ideas	Explanation
The wrong drinks served	mixed up our drink order made a mistake with our drink order
A waiter or waitress being rude to you	

You must be able to answer these questions:

When   ... did you receive this bad service? (*e.g. date, time of day*)
Where   ... did you receive this bad service? (*e.g. name, address of place*)
Who   ... gave you this bad service? (*e.g. use the name of this person if you know it*)
What   ... was this bad service? Explain. (*e.g. describe what happened*)
How   ... do you want the person you're writing to, to deal with this?
             (*e.g. do you want an apology, a refund, something else?*)

To complain about a faulty product

Format: your letter of complaint

Paragraph 1	Your first sentence must let the reader know why you are writing.
I am writing to inform you about …	
	Explain the details of your complaint, e.g. Where? When?
I visited your … on … at … *I purchased … on … at …*	
	Express your disappointment.
I am disappointed with/about …	
Paragraph 2	Explain the details of your complaint further.
The service I received was … because … *The product I purchased was … because …*	
	e.g. What? How?
Paragraph 3	Explain what you want this person to do.
I am hoping you can resolve this matter by …	
	If you want a refund, a replacement or an apology, then tell them this. Provide your phone number and/or email address (optional).

You must be able to answer these questions:

When … did you purchase this product? (*e.g. date, time of day*)
Where … did you purchase this product? (*e.g. store name and address*)
What … is wrong with the product? (*e.g. is it faulty? Describe the fault*)
How … do you want the person you're writing to, to deal with this?
           (*e.g. do you want a refund or a replacement?*)

Personal correspondence by electronic mail (email)

Technological improvements in the last several decades have meant that most of us have access to computers and email. Along with this, guidelines have been developed for this new form of communication. This is reflected in the elements and performance criteria your email letter will be assessed against.

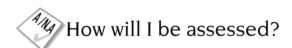 How will I be assessed?

Writing
Elements and performance criteria for Unit Standard 10792
Write formal personal correspondence.

Element 2
Write formal personal correspondence by electronic mail (e-mail).

Performance criteria
2.1   The message is addressed to the intended person, and the subject is clearly stated in the subject line.
2.2   The information presented is accurate, clear, relevant, and ordered in a sequence which fits the context.
2.3   Information is presented so that the content, vocabulary, and tone fit the context, subject matter, and audience.
2.4   Punctuation is accurate in terms of full stops, capital letters, and commas.
2.5   Spelling is accurate at least 90% of the time.
2.6   The form of address used fits the context and the relationship between writer and audience.

Writing your email letter

Your purpose: to thank or invite someone.
Your audience: the person you're inviting or thanking
   e.g. a friend or family member.
Your topic: one of the following:
* to thank someone for something they have done, given to you or helped you with
* to invite a friend to an event.

 Note: Before you begin your own email, your teacher will provide you with an exemplar of an email which has passed the marking criteria for this unit standard.

Format : your email letter

Paragraph 1	Explain your purpose – your reason for writing.
Paragraph 2	Provide the necessary details. For an invitation make sure you include the what, when, where, who, why and how. Express an interest to see this person again, possibly at the event you've invited them to or express your thanks if your purpose is to thank them.

Email writing procedure

To:	The email address of the person you're writing to.
Cc:	The addresses or other email addresses you may be sending this email to.
Subject:	What your email is about.

Hi *(their name)*
First paragraph

Second paragraph

Regards
Your name

Email guidelines

While we have particular guidelines (conventions) for traditional letters, we also have some conventions when it comes to writing email letters.

The dos and don'ts of emailing

- Email writing is less formal than traditional post letter writing.
- Do write **to** the receiver's email address.
- Make sure you begin your email with an introduction.
  e.g. Hi Mr Smithers   *– This is acceptable for email writing.*
- Do briefly state your **subject**. This lets someone know what your email will be about.
  e.g. my birthday party
- Make sure you end your email with a sign off. 'Yours sincerely' isn't necessary.
  e.g. Regards or Kind regards *– This is a polite and friendly way to sign off.*
- Then write your name underneath.
- Don't write in capitals – it makes it look as if you're shouting and it's less easy to read.
- Don't write anything you wouldn't be prepared to say in public.

▌ Useful tip

The **cc** line is used when you're sending copies of your email to other people. The recipient (the person receiving it) can see who else has been sent the same email. A carbon copy is an exact copy, so each person in the cc column will receive the exact same email. cc is an abbreviation for '*Carbon copy*'.

The **Bcc** line is used when you're sending copies of your email to other people but they can't see who else has been sent the same email. Bcc means '*blind carbon copy*'.

UNIT 2 Reading texts for practical purposes

Unit Standard 2977: what is it all about?

For this unit standard you will need to read at least three texts for practical purposes.
This assessment will be given to you in class and you will be given several periods to complete it. You will have the opportunity to re-do any answers you get incorrect the first time.

What is a text?

A text is anything that communicates a message. It usually has words and can be in spoken, written or visual form.

Read means to *'extract meaning'*. Reading is a skill we practise everyday.

- We read things all the time, whether deliberately or unconsciously. Think of all the texts you read between waking up and arriving at school, e.g. reading the time on your alarm clock, the label on the tube of toothpaste, street signs on the way to school.
- Deliberate reading is what we do when we pick up a book, a magazine or a newspaper.
- Unconscious reading is what our brains naturally do. As soon as we are born our brains are deciphering shapes and patterns, without even thinking about it. And, once we learn to read we look for meanings in the shapes and patterns of written language.

Working out what we already know

- What are some common texts?
- What are their purposes?
- What is a practical purpose?
- What does it mean to read a text for a practical purpose?

Use your own knowledge and a dictionary to answer the questions above.

 ## How will I be assessed?

This unit standard is worth four credits.

You will sit a three-part assessment by answering questions about the three texts which will be provided for you. You need to pass the whole assessment to earn your four credits.

This assessment follows the elements and performance criteria for 2977.

Although this unit standard is from the sub-field of Communication Skills, the four credits are still literacy credits.

Reading
Elements and performance criteria for Unit Standard 2977
Read texts for practical purposes.

Element 1
Read texts for practical purposes.

Range: at least three texts

Performance criteria
1.1   The purpose of the text is identified in terms of subject.
1.2   Main points and/or main text sections are summarised in terms of content.
1.3   Specific information is located in the text to meet the practical purpose.
1.4   Abbreviations and/or technical words used are interpreted according to the purpose of the text.
1.5   Any prior knowledge of the subject is identified in terms of linking the information in the text.

Note: Texts referred to in this unit standard:
- could include: training handouts, forms, directions, signs, notices, messages, notes, labels, classified advertisements, advertisements, minutes, promotional material, incident reports, business letters, job descriptions, and newspapers, telephone directories and dictionaries;
- could have: complementary illustrations or diagrams;
- do not incorporate: complex language and structures.

Getting started

Two key words you will need to know for this assessment are **purpose** and **subject**.
- A **purpose** is the reason for something. For example, the purpose of school is to teach you how to learn and to earn qualifications which will help you get a job in the future.

The purpose of a text is the reason why it was created.
- A **practical purpose** is a reason for something which is useful and realistic.

Task: What are the purposes of the following texts? For each text ask yourself: 'What was the text created for?'
1   A map
2   A danger sign
3   A name badge
4   A car advertisement.

When looking for the purpose of a text we also need to identify the subject.
- The **subject** of a text is what the text is actually about. For example, the subject of the White Pages is the phone numbers of people in a particular city.

Task: Now that you have come up with purposes for the four texts listed above, decide on a subject for each.

Task: Read the description for each of the following texts, then decide on the subject and purpose.
1   A non-fiction book in the Teenage section of the public library, called *101 things you need to know about rugby league.*
2   A pamphlet called *Recycling your paper and cardboard* delivered to mailboxes.
3   A bus timetable for the Wellington central city area, with a map and a timetable.
4   A map of Hamilton, including street names and local schools and churches.

Text activities

Task: Group task

First, discuss the following texts within your group and write down your first thoughts about each of these texts. Then answer the questions below. Make sure you read each of the four texts carefully.

Text 1: Netsafe's anti text-bullying pamphlet

Messaging
• Before sending a TXT, PXT or Video-PXT ask yourself if you would be happy to receive such a message. If the answer is no, don't send it.
• If someone took a PXT or Video-PXT of you without your knowledge and sent it on, you might be upset. So, don't do it to someone else. Ask if it's okay before you take a PXT.
• Don't use language or pictures that might upset or offend people.

Want more info?
For more information on TXT, PXT, Video-PXT, chatroom and internet safety, check out **www.netsafe.org.nz** or **www.vodafone.co.nz** (under About Vodafone, Responsible Mobile Use). Or you can call NetSafe or Vodafone on the numbers below.

* PXT is a registered Vodafone trademark.

NetSafe
The Internet Safety Group
(0508 638 723)

vodafone
(0800 800 021)

TXT BULLY

If someone is picking on you via your mobile, call NetSafe on 0508 NETSAFE and (638 723) they'll help you out.

Netsafe and Vodafone

How to get the bully off your back

It may not feel like it, but there are loads of things you can do to help stop and prevent bullying on your mobile.

You are not alone

Firstly, don't feel you have to deal with it by yourself - tell your friends and parents or call toll-free **0508 NETSAFE (0508 638 723)**. They're a New Zealand organisation helping to keep you safe, and they're friendly and easy to talk to.

What can Vodafone do?

If necessary there's a number of things Vodafone can do to help, like warning the bully, switching you to a new number or even barring the bully from our network. We can do it, so give us a call if you need to.

Two key suggestions to help stop TXT bullying

1. Be super careful about who you give out your number to (and don't give it to people you don't know).
2. If you get a TXT from an unknown number do not reply to it.

Parents can help... they really can!

If there's a problem with someone constantly sending you messages that upset or offend you, tell your parents or a trusted adult. Together, you should be able to work out how to knock any problem on the head before it gets out of hand.

What can you do?

• Be very careful about giving out your personal details via mobile to anyone you don't know (and don't give out someone else's number without asking first).

• If you get a TXT or PXT* that makes you feel uncomfortable, do not reply.

• If you regularly get TXTs or PXTs that upset you, tell someone you trust. If they are life-threatening, call the police immediately.

• Vodafone has various options for blocking nuisance TXT and PXT messages that you don't want.

• Call Vodafone free on **777** from your mobile with the message details. Remember, do not reply to a threatening or harassing message.

• If you use chat services, remember people may not be who they say they are.

• Once you have your chat nickname, that's all other chatters will see. They can only find out your mobile number and personal details if you tell them.

• Remember when you choose a chat nickname that people may judge what kind of person you are by the 'tone' of that name.

• If you get into conversations or receive messages you're uncomfortable with, you can send the **IGNORE** command to **220** to stop receiving TXT chat messages from that chatter.

1   What is the subject of this text? What is the text about?
2   What is the purpose of this text?
3   Who is the target audience for this text? Who should be reading it?
4   What is text bullying? Why is it a problem?
5   Who is responsible for this advertisement?
6   What can Vodafone do to help you if you're being text bullied?

Text 2: 'AA Driver Training' advertisement

1 What is the subject of this text? What is the text about?
2 What is the purpose of this text?
3 Who is this advertisement aimed at?
4 Who is responsible for this advertisement?
5 Why do the AA think you should choose them?

Text 3: Connect to the circuit pamphlet

1 What is the subject of this text? What is the text about?
2 What is the purpose of this text?
3 Who is this advertisement aimed at?
4 Why is a map included in this pamphlet?
5 What does 'Connect to the Circuit' mean?

Text clues

When we read a text we need to pay attention to the clues it gives us. The first step is identifying a **subject** and a **purpose**.
The next steps are to identify the:

- context;
- layout; and
- language.

Context

Context means 'where something comes from'.

- Where a text is made or distributed is the context.
- The words directly before and after a particular sentence are also the context. This context can give us clues about what is being said in this sentence.

Layout

Layout is how a text is **set out** or **positioned**. This can tell us a lot about the text.

Think about how the writing is set out. What sizes and fonts are used for the lettering? Are there any pictures or diagrams used? What colours are used? Are any bullet points used? Where has each block of written language been placed?

Language

Language refers to the **words used** in a text.

The most important words are called **key words**. We can identify the key words by picking out the ones that are needed the most in a sentence. For example, in the following sentence:

When we read a text we need to pay attention to the clues it gives us.

the **key words** are: *read, text, pay, attention, clues* and *gives*. The smaller words are used to make this sentence make sense but they are less important than the key words.

Are any abbreviations used? Are any technical or specialised words used?

 Task: Your homework task is to bring a text to class tomorrow, e.g. a pamphlet, advertisement, magazine, flyer, mailer.

Language

The language used in texts is important because it lets us know what a text is about. Two things you need to know about are:

- technical words; and
- abbreviations.

Technical words

These are also called jargon or specialised language. Depending on who it is written for, a text may contain some technical or specialised words. For example, a legal text would include technical legal language: affidavit, defendant, prosecutor.

Task: What are some technical words for the following topics?
1   Computer gaming
2   Cellphones

Task: Have a close look at Text 4 and explain what the following words and terms mean:
- apprenticeship
- established
- wheel alignment
- qualification
- automotive.

Text 4: UCOL advertisement

Abbreviations

An **abbreviation** is the **shortened form** of a word or term. For example, Dr is the abbreviation of doctor, St is the abbreviation of street.

Why do we use abbreviation?

1   To save time, when we're taking notes.
2   When we need to shorten the amount of words used.
3   To avoid repetition of lengthy words or terms.

Task: One of the most common uses of abbreviations can be seen in the classified advertisements in newspapers. Have a look at the Classified section of a newspaper and then make up a chart with the following headings to write down the abbreviations you know and those you don't.

Abbreviations I recognise   Abbreviations I want to learn about

Task: What do these common abbreviations mean?

1	aka	2	Wed	3	Rd	4	Ave
5	n/a	6	no.	7	prev.	8	p/a

  Tip

If you use the first and the last letter of a word, you don't need to use a full stop. e.g. Mr = Mister, St = Street and Saint, **but** if only the first letters of a word are used then you need to use a full stop, Maj. = Major.

Task: Match each of the following abbreviations to their meanings.

1   encl.   a   or nearest offer
2   p.t.o.   b   General Practitioner
3   Co.   c   Reverend
4   ono   d   please turn over
5   Rev.   f   company
6   GP   g   enclosed

Task: Text 5: Map of Manukau Institute of Technology

Work with a partner or by yourself to answer the following questions in your English book.

1 What do you **already know** about:
   - maps
   - Manukau
   - M.I.T.?

2 Look closely at the text. What is the **purpose** of this text?

3 What do the following abbreviations mean when used in this text?
   a Rd
   b Pl
   c Res
   d Ave
   e NB
   f W
   g G
   h 14

4 Why do you think there are so many abbreviations used on this map, e.g. A, C, D, NA, NB, NC...?

5 Imagine you are on Alexander Crescent by the Student Village at Gate 15 and you need to get to the Technology Administration building. Look closely at the map and then write down the instructions about how to get there. Make sure you provide street names and directions such as *left* and *right*.

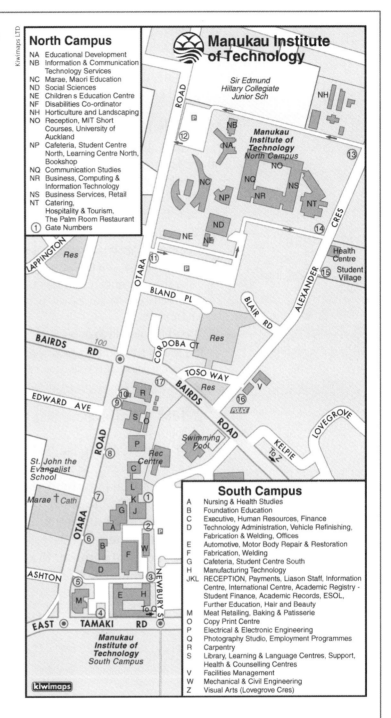

Kiwimaps LTD

North Campus
NA Educational Development
NB Information & Communication Technology Services
NC Marae, Maori Education
ND Social Sciences
NE Children s Education Centre
NF Disabilities Co-ordinator
NH Horticulture and Landscaping
NO Reception, MIT Short Courses, University of Auckland
NP Cafeteria, Student Centre North, Learning Centre North, Bookshop
NQ Communication Studies
NR Business, Computing & Information Technology
NS Business Services, Retail
NT Catering, Hospitality & Tourism, The Palm Room Restaurant
① Gate Numbers

Manukau Institute of Technology

Sir Edmund Hillary Collegiate Junior Sch

Manukau Institute of Technology North Campus

South Campus
A   Nursing & Health Studies
B   Foundation Education
C   Executive, Human Resources, Finance
D   Technology Administration, Vehicle Refinishing, Fabrication & Welding, Offices
E   Automotive, Motor Body Repair & Restoration
F   Fabrication, Welding
G   Cafeteria, Student Centre South
H   Manufacturing Technology
JKL RECEPTION, Payments, Liason Staff, Information Centre, International Centre, Academic Registry - Student Finance, Academic Records, ESOL, Further Education, Hair and Beauty
M   Meat Retailing, Baking & Patisserie
O   Copy Print Centre
P   Electrical & Electronic Engineering
Q   Photography Studio, Employment Programmes
R   Carpentry
S   Library, Learning & Language Centres, Support, Health & Counselling Centres
V   Facilities Management
W   Mechanical & Civil Engineering
Z   Visual Arts (Lovegrove Cres)

Manukau Institute of Technology South Campus

kiwimaps

Summarising

Often when we are reading texts for practical purposes we will need to look for essential information in the text. This is called **summarising**.

To 'summarise' means to make a summary of something – a shortened version of the main ideas. We can do this by finding the most important words and ideas, which are called **key words.** By pulling out the key words we can summarise the text.

Methods of making a summary

There are four summarising methods. For some texts you will need to use one, for others you may need to use a few.

1   Look closely at the headings and subheadings.

    These give us clues about where to look for specific information, but headings don't always lead us to the information we want.

2   Scan the text by moving your eyes across each line to look for key words.

    Scanning is faster than reading the whole text, especially when you get good at it.
    However, if you scan too fast you might miss the key words you're looking for.

3   Use the contents and index pages (when applicable).

    This works well for whole books or large texts, but usually shorter texts don't have contents or index pages.

4   Read the whole text.

    This is good for short texts because this means you won't miss any key words.
    However, if your text is very long this may take too much time.

Task: Which summarising method or methods would you use for the following?

1   **Practical purpose:** To find out how to get from Rotorua to Taupo.
    Text: New Zealand Road Atlas.

2   **Practical purpose:** To find a part time job.
    Text: The Classified advertising section of your local newspaper.

3   **Practical purpose:** To find a hotel to stay at on a visit to Christchurch.
    Text: The YellowPages

4   **Practical purpose:** To find out information about a specific course?
    Text: Tertiary education prospectus

Practice assessment

Text 6: ASB advertisement

1 What do you **already know** about:
- banks e.g. ASB
- banking
- tertiary package?

Now read Text 6.

2 What is the **purpose** of this text?

3 Imagine you are on a tertiary course and you are interested in opening a bank account with ASB. List the three ways you can do this.

4 Identify two benefits of the ASB tertiary account.

5 The words '*Beans, bread, buckeroos, cash, coin, dough, loot, green stuff, lucre, mazuma, moolab*' all have the same meaning. What is it?

6 Select three of the following technical words and terms. Explain what they mean when they are used in this text.

Zero EFTPOS fees	Student Survival Pack	Tertiary Package
No monthly account fee	lending criteria	overdraft

7 Explain what the following abbreviations mean.

a %

b ASB

c EFTPOS

Final assessments

You will find the images for more assessments below and in the colour section at the end of the book. Your teacher will introduce these assessments.

- **Assessment A:** Polyfest map – see colour section.
- **Assessment B:** OPC advertisement – page25.
- **Assessment C:** WSPA advertisement – see colour section.

Assessment B: OPC advertisement

OUTER LIMITS

www.opc.org.nz

OUTDOOR ADVENTURES

INCREASE PERSONAL CONFIDENCE AND AWARENESS THROUGH ACHIEVEMENT, GROUP WORK AND FUN, WHILE LEARNING SKILLS USED IN THE OUTDOORS.

OPC's Adventure Challenge programmes give you the chance to tackle adventures in the mountains, bush, rivers and lakes of the Central Plateau. Visit some amazing places and learn more about yourself along the way.

YOUTH ADVENTURE CHALLENGE – FIVE DAYS (14 to 18 year-olds)

- Local adventures – group games, initiative activities, rock climbing, abseiling, tramping, challenge ropes course, orienteering and caving.
- Mountain adventures – climb a volcanic peak or rock on the cliffs of Tongariro National Park.
- Water adventures – The summer programme offers kayaking, canoeing, gorging, or white water tube rafting.
- Expedition – tramp, climb or paddle on an overnight adventure, spend the night out under flies or in tents.
- December 12 – 16 '05
- December 19 – 23 '05
- January 16 – 20 '06

Scholarships are available for courses, contact OPC to see if you are eligible.

For more information and an application form, visit our website at www.opc.org.nz, email opc@opc.org.nz, or phone 07 386 5511.

www.opc.org.nz

www.outwardbound.co.nz

www.spiritofadventure.org.nz

UNIT 3 Wide reading

Unit Standard 8808: what is it all about?

Over the course of this year, you will need to read at least six written texts. For each of the six texts you select and read, you will need to write a reading log.

What is a reading log?

- This is where you write a record of your personal response. Your personal response is what you thought about the text.
- Each text review you write must be about your own thoughts, feelings and ideas.
- You will also need to refer to at least two specific details from the text you read. This is stated in the marking criteria on the next page. You need to include specific details so your teacher can clearly see that you have read the text and have been able to respond to or discuss specific details.

What's a written text?

A text communicates a message. A written text is a particular kind of text. A written text is a text designed for us to read, as it is made up (mostly) of words.

There are many types of written text, for example, a short story, a novel …

Working out what we already know

- List all the written text types you can think of.
- List all the authors you can think of.
- List all the texts you have read or would like to read.

How will I be assessed?

This unit standard is worth three credits.

The six reading logs you will need to write for this unit will be assessed by the following elements and performance criteria. Each log must meet these criteria.

English written language
Elements and performance criteria for Unit Standard 8808
Read an inclusive range of written texts and record the reading experience.

Element 1
Read an inclusive variety of written texts and record the reading experience.

Range: at least six written texts from at least two different categories.

Categories may include contemporary novel, pre-20th century text, collection of short stories, drama, poetry, anthology, extended magazine articles, biographies, reference books, websites.

Performance criteria
1.1   Selection includes more than one cultural perspective and has regard to gender balance.
1.2   Reading includes at least one text with an established critical reputation.
1.3   Reading log records date of main entry, gives title and writer or source of each text, and a brief personal response with specific reference to details of each text.
1.4   Evidence of texts having been read is demonstrated for at least one random sample text recorded in the reading log.

Range: evidence of text having been read could be through discussion, or other appropriate written, oral, or visual form.

Guidelines for Unit Standard 8808

From your reading selection you must make sure you have included:
- texts from **at least one** text type, for example, one novel, one biography, two extended magazine articles and two short stories.
- **gender balance** – a mix of both male and female authors.
- **more than one cultural perspective** – texts written by authors from a particular cultural viewpoint, for example, a novel about a Maori perspective (point of view) by a Maori author or a short story by a Samoan author, from a Samoan perspective.
- at least one text with **an established critical reputation.** Evidence of this might be a text which has won an award.

What happens once I've finished reading a text?
- Once you have read a text, draft out your reading log in your English book.
- Aim to write at least half a page per reading log. This is explained in more detail on the next page.
- Proofread your reading log draft and then ask your English teacher to check that you're on the right track. When you're both happy with your reading log, write your good copy.

Getting started

Reading logs

For each written text you read, you need to complete a reading log. This is begun by filling in the following criteria about your text.

Title

The name of the text.

Author or source

The author is the writer of the text. Sometimes texts like extended magazine articles or webpages don't appear to have an author. When you find this, you'll need to write down the **source** of the text. For a magazine this will be the magazine title and the date. For a webpage, the source is the website address.

Text type

The type of written text, for example, a short story, a novel, a biography …

Cultural perspective

This means that at least two of your six texts should be from a different cultural point of view, for example, a newspaper article about an Asian person who has achieved something, from his cultural point of view.

Personal response

This is the part where you get to say what you thought about the text you read. Make sure you include **at least two** specific examples to support your opinion. A specific example may be:

- a detail or example of something that happened
- a quote. Select an important sentence or two and use quotation (speech) marks.

> Your teacher will provide you with exemplars; these are reading logs that have or have not met the marking criteria for this unit standard.

Tips

- Do not retell the story.
- Do not copy information from the blurb of a text.

What is an established critical reputation?

You need to read *at least one text* that has an established critical reputation.

- A **reputation** is what people think about something; it refers to the quality and status of someone or something.
- To be **critical** means to look closely and make judgements about something. When we look critically at a text we are judging it.
- Therefore; a **critical reputation** means that a text has been judged by many readers over time and is still well-known and respected. This means that it has been accepted by the critics.
- To be **established** means to be already set in place. A text that is established is one that is time honoured and recognised.

  So, a text with an **established critical reputation** is one which is well-known, widely read and has received positive criticism over time. It will:

- have a review of the text in a magazine or newspaper; or
- have a recommendation from another author; or
- be a text from a classical author;
- a text that has reprinted many times and continues to be popular; or
- be a text which has been nominated for, or has won an award.

Check with your teacher if you're not sure whether your text has an established critical reputation. Another thing you could do is photocopy the evidence and attach it to your reading log, e.g. a newspaper review of the text.

Prompts

Once you've read a written text, you've usually got a clear idea of what you think about it. But what do you write?

Here are some prompts that may help get you thinking about your written text. Using one or more of these prompts can help you focus on:

- what you thought of the written text and why
- recalling specific details from the written text.

The key is to identify which parts of the text you liked (or disliked) and explain by giving reasons why.

Character

- A character I felt I could relate to was … I felt I could relate to him/her because …
- A character I admired was … because …
- A character I disliked was … because …
- A character I found memorable was …. I found him/her memorable because …
- A character/person I learnt from was …. I learnt …
- An important relationship in this text was … I thought it was important because …

Theme

- A main theme/idea in this text was …
- One thing I learnt from reading this text was …
- An important message in this text was ….. I think it was important because …
- I liked/disliked the main idea in this text because …
- An important conflict in this text was … It was important because …

General

- The cover/title/illustration attracted me to this text because …
- I really enjoyed the ending/beginning of this text because …
- The way this text was told/narrated was interesting because …
- A sentence which really inspired me was … because …
- I found parts of this text … in particular when …
- I really enjoyed this text because …
- This text had a … cultural perspective; this was clear from …
- This text had an established critical reputation; this was clear from …

UNIT 4 Static image

Unit Standard 12417: what is it all about?

For this unit standard you will need to produce a static image.

What is a static image?

Static means *still* and an **image** is a *picture*. So a **static image** is a *still picture*.

- The purpose of a static image is to communicate a meaning.
- A static image is a visual text and there are many types of static images, for example a photograph, storyboard …

The static image you will be producing needs to be planned out. You will be required to use visual features and verbal features.

- The word *visual* relates to vision and viewing; visual features are the parts of a static image which make up the image, the pictures, for example colour, borders, layout …
- The word *verbal* relates to words verbalised (said) or written down. Verbal features are imperatives, personal pronouns, metaphors …

Working out what we already know

- List all the types of static image you can think of.
- List all the examples of static images you can think of.
- What visual features do you know about?
- What verbal features do you know about?
- How do you think visual and verbal features are combined in static images?

How will I be assessed?

This unit standard is worth two credits.

The static image you will need to produce for this unit standard will be assessed by the following elements and performance criteria.

English visual language
Elements and performance criteria for Unit Standard 12417
Present a static image using verbal and visual features.

Element 1
Present a completed static image, or image at a pre-production stage, using verbal and visual features.

Range: includes at least one static image chosen from categories such as: cartoon, static image representing an idea in another text, billboard, advertisement, product packaging, stage set, storyboard, newspaper pages, news story with accompanying photograph and caption, web page.

Performance criteria
1.1　Presentation of visual and verbal features communicates ideas or relates narrative.

Range: at least one verbal and one visual feature;
- visual language features could include use of colour, style or lettering, symbolism;
- verbal language features could include words used, figures of speech, grammatical structures.

1.2　Presentation demonstrates production techniques appropriate to form and purpose.

A/NA

What are visual features?

Visual features are visual elements. *Visual* relates to *vision*, to what we see, so the word visual is about pictures. Visual features relate to how a static image is presented, and how it looks. A static image is often made up of both verbal and visual features.

　　Read the following list of visual features. You may choose to use some of these when producing your own static image.

Colour

- Colours can be used to catch our attention or to communicate a meaning.
- For more details about how colour can be used, refer to Communicating with colour on page 33.

Contrast

- When two 'opposite' colours are used together this can create a contrast, for example black and white, black and yellow.
- Contrast is used to attract our attention or to suggest a deeper meaning between two sides or two parts of a whole.
- Contrast is also used to show opposites in written texts.

Layout

This is the way all the parts of a static image are arranged or laid out. The layout is an important part of planning a static image because the way parts are set out can help to communicate meaning.

Dominant feature

The word *dominant* means the biggest or strongest, so a dominant feature is the biggest, most visible or obvious part of a static image.

Usually the dominant image will be the part that catches your eye first. It may be a picture, an image or words.

Lettering

The lettering or font used for any writing in a static image must suit the static image. There are many styles of lettering to choose from: you only have to take a look at the fonts you can select from in Word on a computer.

Shape

The shapes used within a static image can help communicate ideas. The shape of the dominant feature can be used to make sure all parts of the static image fit together.

Proportion

The word *proportion* means size in relation to all parts of a static image. The sizes you use for the parts of a static image help determine the importance of the different parts in relation to other parts. The most important part is often the largest and this can be a dominant feature such as a message or an image.

Symbolism

A symbol is something (usually an object) which represents or stands for something else. Depending on how they are used, symbols can represent different things. For example, a gun can represent danger and violence, while a light shining through darkness can represent hope.

Borders

A border is a frame around a part or the whole of a static image. Borders are used to focus a viewer's attention on what is inside the frame. There are many different styles of borders. When using borders you must make sure the style of the border you choose suits your static image.

Balance

A static image must be balanced. By thinking of your static image in terms of halves, thirds or even quarters you can make sure each part is planned. Each part of your static image needs to add to its meaning.

Note: However; you can use empty white space as a visual feature. Empty space can be used to draw attention to other more important parts of a static image, to highlight them. For example, in the Stop sign used on our roads the empty white space makes the red triangle easier to see.

One way of deciding whether a static image is effective or not is to ask: Does it have impact? Impact is the effect a static image has on the viewer. A static image can have impact if it combines visual and verbal features and it has a clear message or main idea.

Communicating with colour

Like certain objects or ideas, colours can also act as symbols. Depending on how they're used, colours can represent different ideas.

The use of colours in a static image can have particular connotations. A **connotation** is the feeling or emotional meaning attached to a word, colour or image. For example, a static image about violence and death would use the colour black to help show the connotations of seriousness, sadness and loss. However, a static image about a celebration would use the colour yellow to help show the connotation of happiness.

Black can represent:

violence	darkness	depression	death	evil	war

White can represent:

innocence	cleanliness	emptiness

Red can represent:

love	survival	anger	energy	blood	passion

Blue can represent:

peace	sadness	cold	calmness

Green can represent:

nature	jealousy	balance	newness

Yellow can represent:

happiness	friendship	cowardice

Orange can represent:

creativity	hunger	an accident

Purple can represent:

healing	loneliness	royalty

Gold can represent:

winning	richness	success

What are verbal features?

Verbal features are verbal parts or elements of a static image. *Verbal* relates to **words that are spoken** (verbalised) or written down.

Static images are usually made up of visual and verbal features.

The following is a list of verbal features you may choose to use when producing your own static image. In your static image you must include a quote from the text you have studied. This quote might include one of the following verbal features.

Alliteration

Alliteration occurs when the vowel or consonant letters or sounds are repeated at the start of words written or spoken closely together. This is used to create a particular sound or to make a phrase more memorable or catchy.
Example: She was **c**ool, **c**alm and **c**ollected.

Emotive language

Emotive language uses words that are deliberately chosen to make the audience feel a certain emotion.

To make something like a new soft drink sound exciting and attractive you could use the emotive words: *new, thirst quenching, thrilling, enjoyable …*

To make us feel sympathy for someone like a starving child, you could use the emotive words: *pain, poverty, suffering …*

Hyperbole

A huge exaggeration. This is usually used to emphasise (or underline) an idea.
Example: I'm so hungry, I could eat a horse!

Imperative

A command. This is usually used to force an audience to take action.
Example: Buy now! – '*buy*' is the imperative because it is the verb which tells us what to do.

Personal pronouns

Personal pronouns such as *you* and *your* are often used to directly address the audience, to make them feel more involved.
Example: **You** know **you** want some!
    Personal pronouns such as *we* and *them* can be used to create opposing sides.
Example: **We** understand. **We** know you don't want to lose out like **them**.

Rhetorical questions

These are questions which don't require an answer – the answer is already assumed. A game show host might ask an audience 'Are we ready to start?'. This is rhetorical as the audience are seated and waiting for the game to start, so obviously the answer 'yes' is assumed. Rhetorical questions are asked to gain the audience's attention or to make an audience feel involved.
Example: Who wouldn't want a million dollars?

Repetition

If certain words or phrases are used again this is usually done for emphasis, to highlight important words.
Example: 'When you send in this coupon you'll receive all of this **for only $29.99**. Yes, that's right, all of the pictured CDs **for only $29.99**.'

Simile

This is a comparison which suggests that one thing is similar to another. A simile uses *like* or *as* to compare.
Example: Grace acts **like** an angel. Timmy was as quiet **as** a mouse.

Metaphor

This is a comparison which takes one step further than a simile. It compares two things by saying one thing *is* actually another.
Example: Grace **is** an angel. Timmy **was** a mouse.

Statistics

Facts and statistics are used to make something sound more important, more authoritative.
Example: **Four in five people** regularly buy this product!

Task: Te Mana static image

Look at the Te Mana advertisement in the colour section at the end of the book. Look closely at this static image and then answer the following questions in your English book.

1   What is the purpose of this static image?
2   Who is the target audience and how do you know this?
3   What is the dominant feature?
4   *'To honour the past we must prepare for the future.'* What does this mean?
5   Identify two visual features used in this static image and explain why they have been used.
6   Identify one verbal feature used in this static image and explain why it has been used.

Task: Life or Death static image

Look closely at the static image on page 36 to identify the visual and verbal features used. Answer these questions in your English book.

1   What is the purpose of this static image?
2   Who is the target audience?
3   What is the dominant feature?
4   Identify **two** visual features used in this static image and explain why they have been used, for example, *colours, contrast, lettering, proportion, shapes, symbols, borders, balance, empty space.*
5   Identify **one** verbal feature used in this static image and explain why it has been used, for example, *metaphor, simile, use of statistics, repetition, rhetorical questions, personal pronouns, imperative, hyperbole, alliteration, emotive language.*

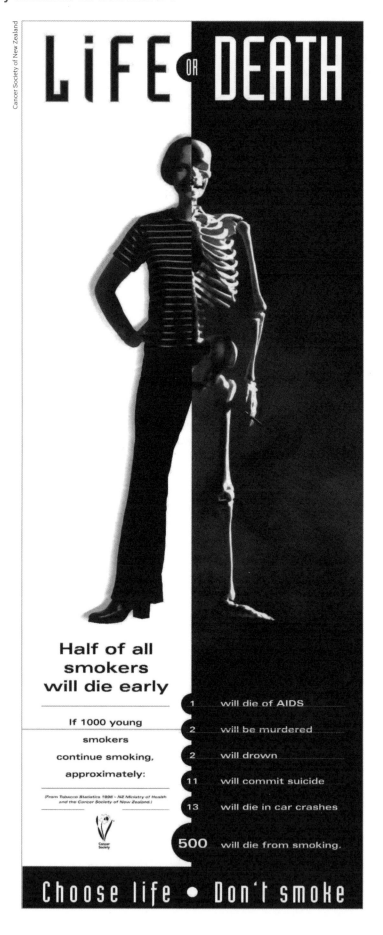

Producing your static image

For any text you are developing it is important to know who your audience is and what your topic and purpose are.

When developing your static image you need to be aware of:

Audience: your teacher, other teenagers

Topic: an important idea from the text you have studied

Purpose: to communicate a message or main idea from your text.

 ## Assessment: producing a static image

For this assessment you will need to plan, design and produce a static image about the text you have studied in class. This static image will be in the form of an A3-sized poster (unless your teacher advises you otherwise).

The static image you produce will need to be about the text you have studied in class.

- Your purpose is to communicate a main idea from this text, through your own static image.
- You will also need to complete a written commentary (your teacher will show you how to set this out). This is an explanation of your static image, it is a way of explaining your static image.
- Select a sentence which helps to explain the main idea you are communicating. This is your quote and should be included as part of your static image.
- Plan your static image carefully and check with your teacher before you begin your good copy on A3 paper.

> Make sure you have thought about :
> – the visual features you will use
> – the verbal features you will use.
> Make sure you have read the performance criteria for 12417 on page 31 and understand how you will be assessed.

 Task: Fill in the written commentary form your teacher will give to you.

 Task: Copy out the following chart so you can check your progress as you plan your static image.

1 I have planned and designed a static image using my own ideas.	
2 I have used at least one visual feature, e.g. colour, style, lettering, symbolism.	
3 My visual feature(s) help communicate my main idea.	
4 I have used at least one verbal feature, e.g. words used, figures of speech, grammatical structures.	
5 My verbal feature(s) help communicate my main ideas.	
6 I have used a quote from my studied text in my static image.	
7 My static image is appropriate (suitable) in terms of its purpose.	
8 I have completed my written commentary about my static image.	

UNIT 5 Wide viewing

Unit Standard 8810: what is it all about?

For this unit standard you will need to read at least six visual texts.
For each text you read you will need to write a viewing log

What is a viewing log?

This is where you write your personal response. Your personal response is what you thought about the visual text and why.

- Each viewing log you write must be about your own thoughts, feelings and ideas.
- You will also need to refer to at least two specific details from the text you have viewed.

What is a visual text?

A text is anything that communicates a message. The word *visual* relates to **vision**, to what we see or watch. A visual text is one which may have words or dialogue, but is made up mostly of pictures.

There are many types of visual texts, for example a documentary, an advertisement, a film …

Working out what we already know

- List all the visual text types you can think of.
- Which visual texts do you prefer to watch / view and why?
- List some of your favourite visual texts.

Have another look at this list and then sort it out. For each text you've listed, decide what visual text type it is.

How will I be assessed?

This unit standard is worth two credits.

The six viewing logs you will need to write for this unit standard will be assessed by the following rlements and performance criteria. Each viewing log must meet these criteria.

English visual language
Elements and performance criteria for Unit Standard 8810
Read an inclusive range of visual texts and record the reading experience.

Element 1
Read an inclusive range of visual texts and record the reading experience.

Range: includes at least six visual texts from at least two different categories.

At least one text must be a static image chosen from categories such as posters, advertisements, cartoons, book or magazine or compact disc (CD) covers, visual texts from computers, web pages;

At least one text must be a moving image chosen from categories such as film or video chosen from two different genres, television programmes chosen from two different genres, historical visual text, staged play, website.

Performance criteria
1.1   Texts read include more than one cultural perspective and have regard to gender balance.
1.2   Reading log records date of main entry, gives the title or identifies the source, and name of the author, or director, or artist, or performer, and provides a brief personal response with specific reference to details of each text.
1.3   Evidence of texts having been read is demonstrated for at least one random sample text recorded in the reading log, through discussion, or other appropriate written, oral, or visual form.

A/NA ✓

Getting started

We can divide visual texts into two main categories:
- moving images; and
- static images.

What is a moving image?

Any visual text that moves.
Examples: a movie, a TV programme, an interactive webpage, a computer game …

What is a static image?

Any visual text that does not move. **Static** means *still*.
Examples: a poster, a comic strip, a website, a magazine advertisement.

Why is this important?

For this unit standard you will need to read a mixture of moving visual texts and static moving texts.

Identifying visual texts

Since we're reading written texts for 8808 and reading visual texts for 8810 it is important to keep track of which is which.

Task: Sort the following text types under two columns headed **Written texts** and **Visual texts**.

short story	music video	comic strip
song lyrics	biography	graphic novel
novel	poem	newspaper article
movie	poster	website

Hint: Some of these texts fit into both categories.

Visual texts: static images

When you've finished reading a visual text the first thing you need to write down is what you thought about it.

Things to think about
- Did you enjoy reading / viewing this text? Why? Why not?
- What was the main message in this text?
- What did you learn / find interesting? Provide examples.
- What was the tone (the mood) of the text?

Visual features

This relates to any visual elements used:

colours	dominant feature	lettering	layout	symbols
contrast	borders	balance	proportion	

Verbal features

This relates to any words that were written:

emotive language	imperative	hyperbole	pun	repetition	simile
metaphor		statistics	rhetorical questions	colloquial language	

Colloquial language is the type of English we speak in regular conversations. This is more casual and relaxed than formal language.
Examples: What's up?, See ya, I dunno …

Visual texts: moving images

A moving visual text is a film, TV programme, video cartoon or interactive website.
When reading visual moving texts it is important to be aware of these features.

Camera shots

Close up shot

The screen has a person's whole face and shoulders. This is used to show people's facial expressions. This shot can also give us a close view of an object in the screen.

Mid shot

This shot has one (or more) person's top half (from head to waist usually) in the screen. This is often used to show gestures, movements, facial expressions and relationships of people to each other.

Long shot

This shot is of whole bodies and some of the background can also be seen. This gives us an idea of the action and what is happening. It also lets us see lots of characters and details at once.

Camera angles

High angle

The camera is set high and it is looking down on someone. This is often used to make a person seem small, vulnerable, weak or unimportant.

Low angle

The camera is down low, on the ground. This can be used to make a person or object seem big, dominant or powerful.

Lighting

Back lighting lights up a screen from behind the characters and the action. Spotlights can be used to focus on one person or object. Lighting helps create the mood of a scene. It can also be used to show us the time of day or weather.

Sound

Background music is usually carefully chosen to suit the mood of the action.

Sound effects, such as a drum beating or doors slamming, can be used to build up tension.

Prompts

Once you've read a visual text you need to answer the set questions. The answers you provide for these questions will help you write your viewing log.

Here are some prompts to get you thinking about your visual text. Using one or many of the following prompts will help you to:

- focus on what you thought of the visual text and why
- recall specific details from the visual text.

Static images

1   An important visual feature used was … This was important because …
2   An important verbal feature used was … This was important because …
3   I liked / disliked the layout of this visual text because …
4   I think this visual text was effective because …
5   The dominant feature in this text was … I think this was / wasn't effective because …
6   An important colour used in this text was … This colour was important because …

Moving images

1   An important camera shot used was … This was used when …
2   An important camera angle used was … This was used when …
3   The music used in this visual text was … This worked well because …

General

1   An important idea/message was …
2   This visual text made me feel … because …
3   I really enjoyed this visual text because …
4   The part I liked most about this visual text was …
5   A sentence which really inspired me was … because …
6   A character I could relate to was … I felt I could relate to him/her because …

Viewing log

General questions

1   What was the visual text about?
2   Identify at least two visual features used and explain how/why they were used.
3   Identify at least one verbal feature used and explain how/why it was used.
4   Which part/feature/shot/frame/scene did you like best/least? Explain.
5   Identify an important message/idea/character/setting in the visual text. Explain why it was important.
6   Who is the text targeted at? How do you know this?

 Task: Discuss your answers with another classmate. Then plan and start to draft out your viewing log (your teacher will give you the format). Use the prompts.

Moving image: NZ Army website

Go to www.army.mil.nz and answer the following questions:
1   What is this website about?
2   Do you like the way this website is set out? Comment on the colours used, the lettering, the way links are set out, pictures etc.
3   Explain why the New Zealand army logo is effective.
4   The words: 'Courage, commitment, comradeship, integrity' appear on the Home page of this website. Select two of these and explain why they are important to the army.
5   Select FAQ. What does FAQ mean? Read this section and then identify a piece of information you found interesting.
6   Once you've answered these questions have a go at the Force nine game.

Task: Have a look at the answers you wrote down and discuss these with a partner. Then start drafting out your viewing log. Make sure you express your point of view, what you thought of this website and provide specific examples. You may use the prompts to help you with your viewing log.

Static image: Kapow comic strip

Go to the colour section at the end of the book and read the Kapow comic strip (Visual III).

1   What is the visual text about?
2   How can you tell which words are spoken by characters and which words are part of the captions?
3   a   Describe how Dougie is feeling in frame four.
    b   How is this different from how he is feeling in the last frame, frame nine?
4   Do you think Dougie is a hero? Why? Why not?
5   Frame seven shows a character under water. What clues tell you that he is under water?
6   Which frame did you like the most? Explain.

Task: Have a look at the answers you wrote down and discuss these with a partner. Then start drafting out your viewing log. Make sure you express your point of view, what you thought of this comic strip and provide specific examples. You may use the prompts to help you with your viewing log.

UNIT 6 Research

Unit Standard 8811: what is it all about?

For this unit standard you will need to choose a topic to research, develop key questions and then use a variety of sources to find this information.

Working out what we already know

- What is research?
- Why do people research?
- What are sources?

There are five steps in the research process.
Read the description for each and then decide which order they go in.

Presenting
Answering your key questions and reflecting on your research process.

Processing
Reading and organising the information you have collected. Relating this information to answering your key questions.

Finding
Searching for information from different sources.

Recording
Making notes from the information you find.

Deciding
What is it you want to find information about?

How will I be assessed?

This unit standard is worth three credits.

Your research process and conclusion will be assessed by the following elements and performance criteria.

English written language

Elements and performance criteria for Unit Standard 8811
Collect information using a range of oral, written, and visual sources and methods.

Element 1
Plan the research process.

Performance criteria
1.1 Plan defines research intentions in the form of a research proposal.
Range: the proposal must include but is not limited to research objective (derived from the chosen topic), questions, projected sources (oral, written, visual).

1.2 Planning identifies research methods to be used appropriate to the intention.
Range: select one oral language method such as recording an interview, making notes of a telephone conversation, taping a conversation, listening to a radio or audio recording;
select one visual language method such as viewing a video, using a CD Rom, using the internet;
select two written language methods such as note-taking, designing and administering a questionnaire, designing and carrying out a survey, using a database, using written resources, using a fax machine, using e-mail, writing letters.

Element 2
Collect information related to the research proposal, record the process of collection from the sources used, and discuss the relevance of information collected.

Range: must include oral, written, and visual language sources.

Performance criteria
2.1 Record of collected materials identifies original sources for each item.
2.2 Record of collected materials demonstrates the use of a range of oral, visual and written sources.
2.3 Log records steps taken during process in chronological sequence, and demonstrates use of selected methods to be used.
2.4 Clear, brief written explanation discusses relevance of collected materials to original purpose.

A /N.A

Getting started

 ### Choosing a topic

Researching is an important skill to have in life. It's important in English but you will find that you need to use research skills in other areas too. You need skills like finding information for most tertiary courses and careers as well as for everyday life.

When you are about to choose a topic focus, brainstorm to find an issue you are interested in (e.g. the problem of graffiti in parts of South Auckland).

• Don't pick a topic that is too large (e.g. World War Two).

A topic like this has so much information on it that it could take you years to read information about it.

• Don't pick a topic that is too limited (e.g. limited edition Star Trek memorabilia from 1984).

If a topic is too limited you may have difficulty finding enough information.

Throughout this unit you will get to read exemplars that will show you what to do. These exemplars will help you understand the research process.

Research topic

Once you have narrowed this down to one topic, start brainstorming like this:

Exemplar: brainstorming

and teens   an alternative to doing   types of drinks

'binge drinking' culture   drink driving

Alcohol

drinking age?   what's it made of?

with drugs like marijuana   advertising campaign   alcohol poisoning

Task: Now complete **Part A** of your research booklet. Your teacher will provide the booklet.

Developing key questions

Before you begin to research your topic you need to develop three to four key questions to find out about. Key questions are essential as they are the focus of your research and they give you direction.

Your key questions need to be **open questions**.

- An **open question** is a question that can have any answer; there are no clear limits.

  Example: Why do people enjoy watching sport?

- Avoid **closed questions** as these usually require one word answers, yes or no or a very brief answer.

  Example: What year did the Titanic sink? **Answer:** 1912

Task: Read through the following questions and decide whether they are open or closed questions. For each question write **O** (for open) or **C** (for closed).

1   When did World War one start?
2   How old do you have to be to join the New Zealand Army?
3   Why is the kiwi an endangered species?
4   How is technology changing the way we communicate?
5   Where is Mt Everest?
6   What effects has the depleting ozone layer had on us in New Zealand?

Exemplar
Key question 1: How is binge drinking different from drinking alcohol moderately?
Key question 2: Why do people binge drink?
Key question 3: What effect does binge drinking have on people?

Task: Look closely at the ideas you came up with for your brainstorm. Circle the ones you like and write your three or four key questions in **Part B** of your research booklet.

Fact or opinion?

Most sources you use will provide you with both facts and opinions.

Although both facts and opinions are important when you are researching, it is also important to know the difference between the two.

• A **fact** is a statement which has been proven. It is true.
  Example: Thursday comes after Wednesday.

• An **opinion** is a statement about what someone thinks or feels.
  Example: I love Wednesdays. I hate waking up early each morning.

Task: Read the following statements and decide which are facts and which are opinions. Write **F** (for fact) or **O** (for opinion) in your English book.

1   Wellington is the capital of New Zealand.
2   Holdens are better than Fords.
3   Summer is the best season of the year.
4   Tony scored the highest score in the class.
5   You have to be fifteen to get your driver's licence.
6   Gisborne is the first city on earth to see the sun each day.
7   Geography is the easiest subject.
8   I think Melissa will win the competition.
9   The Southern Cross is on the New Zealand flag.
10   Horror movies are scary.

Planning your sources

When planning your sources, it is important to ask yourself:

- **What** sort of information do I need?
  - oral, visual, written, facts, opinions ...?
- **Where** can I find this information?
  - libraries, museums, Citizen's Advice Bureau, internet ...?
- **Who** can help me find my sources?
  - teachers, librarians, public officials ...?

 Task: Now complete **Part C** and **Part D** of your research booklet.

Sources

A source is a place where we locate information.
There are three types of sources:

- written
- visual
- oral.

Written sources

This type of source is made up mostly of words, e.g. a pamphlet, an encyclopaedia.

Visual sources

This type of source is made up mostly of visuals, pictures, e.g. a documentary, a webpage.

Oral sources

This type of source is made up mostly of spoken words or sounds, e.g. a speech, an audio recording.

 Task: Copy out the following Venn diagram and put the sources in the circle they best fit into.

Clue: Some sources fit into more than one category.

radio programmes	documentaries	speeches	articles
diaries	interviews	websites	CD Roms
surveys	films	encyclopaedias	non-fiction books
pamphlets	biographies	questionnaires	

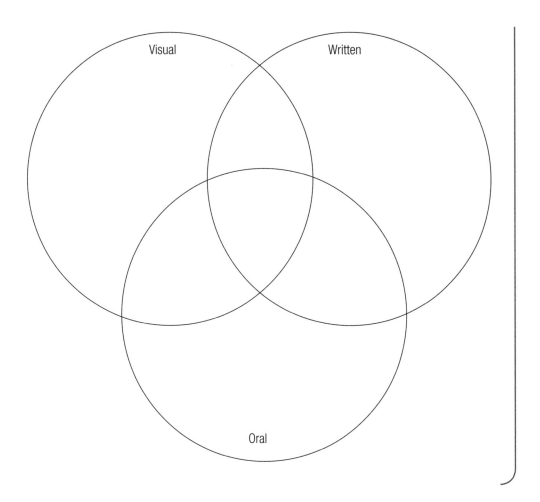

Primary and secondary sources

We know that there are three types of sources but we also need to be aware of primary and secondary sources.

- **Primary sources** are sources that come from people; this is first-hand information.
  Example: an interview.
- **Secondary sources** are second-hand information; this is when someone has got the information from one or many primary sources.
  Example: a non-fiction book.

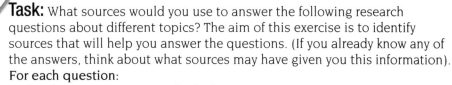

Task: What sources would you use to answer the following research questions about different topics? The aim of this exercise is to identify sources that will help you answer the questions. (If you already know any of the answers, think about what sources may have given you this information).
For each question:
- list **four** sources you can think of;
- **for each source**, decide whether it is a primary source or a secondary source.
  1   Who is Muhammad Ali and why is he famous?
  2   Why is marijuana an illegal drug in New Zealand?
  3   How do blind people find their way around when they can't see?

Identifying key ideas

A key word is an important word. Important words are used to create key (or important) ideas. When we're searching for information we can use key words as clues as they usually lead us to the key ideas.

Exemplar: The key words have already been highlighted for these key research questions.
1 How is **binge drinking** different from drinking **alcohol moderately**?
2 Why do people **binge drink**?
3 What **effect** does **binge drinking** have on people?

 Task: Read the following sentences and then copy down the key words. The first one has been done for you.
1 There are **no species** of **snakes** living in **New Zealand**.
2 The New Zealand flag is made up of the Union Jack and the Southern Cross.
3 The use of cell phones is so widespread now that there are more cell phones than people in this country!
4 The ozone layer above New Zealand and Australia is gradually depleting, this means that the sun is a lot stronger in summer so we need to wear sun screen all the time.
5 Rugby is a popular sport in New Zealand. Our national team, the All Blacks, are world famous.

 Task: Now look at your own key research questions in your research booklet. Highlight or underline the key words. Make sure you use these highlighted key words when you start to search for sources.

Using the internet to research

The internet is information at your fingertips. Although it has only existed since the 1980s, it's worldwide and easy to access.

When you're looking for information on the internet you need to know where to look. The first step is to use a search engine. A search engine is a special programme which helps you find information.

- One of the most popular search engines is Google. You type in your key words and then select from any of the websites they provide you with.
- What other search engines have you used? … heard of?
- If you want to ask a whole question, you might find **Ask Jeeves** at www.askjeeves.com better, as you can type in the whole question.
- Be careful of where you get your information from; it's better to use a more trusted site like www.britannica.com than a website which may have been created in someone's home or for a joke.

Some tips: When using a search engine, you can search the worldwide web (www.) or restrict your source to New Zealand websites only.
- By entering key words you can focus your search.

Exemplar

Key question 1: How is binge drinking different from drinking alcohol moderately?
    Search: *drinking + moderately* (Using + links parts of a search.)
Key question 2: Why do people binge drink?
    Search: *'binge drink'* (Quotation marks can be used to make sure that the whole phrase or term is searched for.)
Key question 3: What effect does binge drinking have on people?
    Search: *binge drinking + effects*

Using the library to research

The library is full of useful sources. It is often the best place to start researching. Most libraries have computer or card catalogues which can help you find information. The librarians can also help you find appropriate sources.

The Non-fiction section

This is arranged according to the Dewey decimal system. All books are arranged from 000 through to 900. Each number represents a different category or topic.

- Non-fiction books are true, factual books. They can provide you with both facts and opinions. For example, a book called 'Climbing Mt Everest' would possibly give you facts about the mountain as well as personal accounts and opinions from experts and climbers.
- When you've found a book, use the **Table of Contents** and the **Index** pages to locate specific information.
  - The Table of Contents is found at the beginning of a book and lists the chapters or sections in a book. It gives us a general idea about what is in the book.
  - The Index page of a book is found at the end of a book. It pinpoints specific parts of the book and refers you to the pages where this information can be found.

The Reference section

Materials in this section cannot be taken out of the library. These sources are a great place to start as they include information on many general topics.

Reference books include encyclopaedias, atlases, dictionaries, almanacs (year books) ...

Vertical file

The vertical file can contain material such as clippings from magazines or newspapers. These are usually filed in alphabetical order in a filing cabinet.

In some instances this information can be more recent. This can be especially useful if you are looking at a current issue. For example, in researching binge drinking you might find more recent information, such as news articles, in the vertical file.

Taking notes

Once you've found a useful source you need to take notes. Taking notes means to find and write down the key ideas that answer your key questions.

How do I take notes?

First you need to find the key ideas. Here are some methods that will help you:

- Use the **headings** and **subheadings** as clues.
  - The **Contents** page of a book lists the chapters.
  - The **Index** page lists the pages where you can find specific information.
- One way to find key ideas is to **skim read**. Skim reading means to make your eyes follow each line of words and stop only for key words.
  - So if you're not reading the whole text (especially when it's very long), skim read for the key words. When you find a key word slow down and carefully read the whole sentence and the sentences around it.
- In the case of visual and oral sources, make sure you take down the key points made.

What do notes look like?

When you take notes follow the format in **Part E** of your research booklet.

Exemplar: Text title: Brain damage from alcohol threatens one Kiwi in five

Author/Source: Martin Johnston, NZ Herald (5/11/07)

Text type: newspaper article

Notes

Key question 1	Key question 2	Key question 3
The World Health Organisation says that more than six drinks in one session is binge drinking – dangerous.	Lack of education about consequences, like brain damage. No routine screening for alcohol-related brain damage in New Zealand.	Brain damage. Can lead to memory loss, difficulty planning, anxiety, paranoia, depression …

Task: Each time you do something for your research make sure that you record this in your research log, **Part G** – Bibliography.

Writing your research report

Once you've finished finding sources, taking notes and recording the process it's time to put all the information together.

- Look closely at the notes you have taken. Identify the information which best answers your key questions.
- Now put these key ideas into your own words to write a paragraph to answer each key question.

Once you have done this, think about your research process and start writing your explanation. Remember the following **performance criteria**.

2.4 ' *Clear, brief written explanation discusses relevance of collected materials to original purpose*'.

Your explanation is where you get to evaluate the research process. This is your opportunity to look back on your research and think about what worked well and what you might have done differently.

Ask yourself these questions:

- Were your materials (sources) relevant to your research topic?
- Were you able to achieve your original purpose – answering your key questions?
- Identify at least one source you used and explain how it was useful.

Task: Now complete **Part H** of your research booklet.

UNIT 7 Transactional writing

Unit Standard 8812: what is it all about?

For this unit standard you will need to produce two pieces of transactional writing.
(Transactional writing can also be called formal writing.)
- Assessment A will be a persuasive essay.
- Assessment B will be an informative news report.

Finding out what we already know

Discuss the following starter sentences with a partner and then complete the sentences.
- Transactional / formal writing is …
- Writing an essay means that you have to …
- Examples of transactional writing are …

What do I write about?
Ideas are the thoughts you have.
Opinions are what you think about ideas, your viewpoint.

Where do I get ideas and information from?
- My own knowledge
- My own opinions and values
- The opinions of my friends and family
- Ideas from newspapers and magazines
- Ideas from TV documentaries or the news.

 How will I be assessed?

This unit standard is worth four credits.

The two pieces of formal writing you will need to produce for this unit standard
will be assessed by the following elements and performance criteria.

English written language
Elements and performance criteria for Unit Standard 8812
Produce transactional written text in simple forms.

Element 1
Produce transactional written text in simple forms.

Range: at least two pieces from any of the following categories – informative writing; persuasive writing, expository writing;

forms could include report writing, speech writing, response to text, review, instructions, letter to the editor.

Performance criteria
1.1   Writing develops idea(s).

1.2   Ideas are logically sequenced and supported by relevant details and / or examples.

1.3   Conventions of chosen form are observed and appropriate to purpose.
Range: conventions could include text organisation, use of sentences, paragraphs, use of language features, literary devices; observing conventions may include deliberately subverting them.

1.4   Final product is crafted to publication standard.
Range: publication standard means that technical accuracy in spelling, punctuation, and syntax is sufficient that the writing could be published in a class or school newspaper or magazine with a few minor alterations.

A/N.A ✓

Getting started

Transactional writing
Two pieces of transactional writing are required for this unit standard.
- The first will be an essay about a topic you're interested in.
- The second will be a news article about an event you've seen.

What are 'transactional written texts in simple form'?
They are pieces of formal writing that meet a particular purpose. Transactional writing can also be called formal writing. Formal language is the type of language you would use when talking to a principal or prospective employer. Writing formally means being polite and not using slang or the contractions of words.

There are three types of formal writing we need to be aware of for this task.

⌐ Informative writing
The purpose of this type of writing is to inform people.
- This could be to inform the general public about important issues or events, like global warming, the result of an All Blacks match or a report on a school play.
- Informative writing is used to write formal reports, reviews and news articles.

⌐ Persuasive writing
The purpose of this type of writing is to persuade people.
- This could be to persuade people to do or not do something or simply to agree with your opinions. You could persuade someone to sponsor you for a race or to support the same political party you do.
- Persuasive writing is used in writing formal reports, news articles, speeches and letters to the editor.

Expository writing

The purpose of this type of writing is to expose (or deliver) information. This could be to provide people with new information or to describe or explain an issue.

Expository writing can be used to write feature articles, formal reports and response to text essays.

Active and passive voices

Active voice

In a sentence the person or thing (noun) doing the action (the verb) is called the subject.

The subject does the action.

Example: Billy caught the ball.

The **verb** is *caught* (to catch) and since Billy caught the ball. *Billy* is the **subject**.

The *ball*, as the **object**, receives the action, has the action done to it.

The active voice is the voice we use in our writing most of the time.

Passive voice

In the passive voice the subject, not the object, receives the action. The subject does the verb while the object does the action.

Tip: Usually we use the conjunction *by* to introduce the passive object.

Example: The ball was **caught** by **Billy**.

      (subject)   (verb) (object)

When should I use the passive voice?

- To make the object seem more important.
- When you don't know what the subject is.

Example: The speech was **delivered** by the **Head girl**.

      (subject)   (verb)   (object)

When you're writing transactionally you can use the passive voice when you are quoting someone.

Task: Read the following sentences and decide whether they are active or passive. Write **A** for active or **P** for passive.

1 Martin mailed the letter this morning.
2 The award was received by Sione.
3 My friend gave me these directions.
4 My dog was walked by the neighbours.
5 He was killed by an armed gunman.

Paragraph writing

A good paragraph follows this format:

    S – statement
    E – explanation
    E – examples

While a question asks the audience to think about a topic, a statement clearly tells the audience what the author already thinks.

Statements

A statement is the sentence that opens a paragraph; it is the first sentence. It must state what the paragraph will be about.

A statement must state your point of view. You can do this by stating 'I agree that ...' or 'I disagree that ...'

Example: Cellphones have changed the way we communicate for the better.

Explanations

The explanation often comes next and this is where you get to explain what your key point is about. Your explanation should explain your statement.

Example: I believe this is a positive change as cellphones have many benefits. Cellphones help us keep in touch with each other and even provide such useful tools as internet access.

Examples

You need examples to persuade people to agree with your point of view. An example acts as evidence. When you show someone evidence they are more likely to agree with you.

What do examples look like?

- An example might be a brief story from your own experience (this is called an anecdote).
- You could provide facts or statistics you've found.

  Example: An overwhelming majority of teenagers own cellphones – well over 70%.

- You could use a quote from someone who holds similar views to you.

Style: persuasive writing

Persuading an audience

How can I make my writing persuasive?

The following techniques can be used to make your essay writing more persuasive.

Using emotive language

Emotive language is words that make us feel a certain emotion or feeling.

- To make us feel **excited** and **enthusiastic** about something we use words like '*bubbly, joyful, fast paced, inspiring*'.

  Example: If you're looking for excitement you should join us for a fast paced adventure!

- To make us feel **pity** and **sympathy** for someone we use words like '*poverty, no chance, misery, suffering*'.

  Example: Their *poverty* and *suffering* is unimaginable.

- You can use emotive words in your essay to persuade your audience to agree with your opinion.

  Example: 'The driving age in New Zealand must be raised. Allowing 15-year-olds to get behind the wheel of a **killing machine** is **irresponsible**.'

Task: List at least four emotive words or phrases you could use to persuade someone to agree with the following statements.

1   They rescued the dog just in time.
    Examples: second chance, cruel attack, survived despite the odds, man's best friend
2   Eating meat is wrong.
3   The hurricane survivors are rebuilding their houses.

Using rhetorical questions

Rhetorical questions are a special type of question. They are asked to create an effect, to make the audience think. It is assumed that everyone knows the answer so a rhetorical question is not meant to be answered.

'Do you think I was born yesterday?' – This rhetorical question may be asked to suggest that the writer isn't gullible or easily fooled, therefore wasn't 'born yesterday'.

Task: Think of a rhetorical question you could use to grab the audience's attention about the following issues.

1   Winning at sport.
2   Achieving your goals.
3   Encouraging people to avoid fast food.

Using personal pronouns

Pronouns are words used in place of nouns. Personal pronouns are pronouns which can be used to help connect with an audience.

*   To include or talk directly to an audience you might use the words '**you**' and '**your**'.
    Example: '*You* need this product. *Your* family's safety is in *your* hands.'
*   To create sides, '**we, us and them,**' can make the reader feel more included.
    Example: '*We* know how to win – not like *them*.'
*   Using personal pronouns is an effective way to address your audience and to persuade them to agree with your point of view. This is useful when you're trying to get an audience to agree with your opinion.

Now think about which of these techniques you could use for your essay.

Planning your essay

Once you've decided on your topic and brainstormed your ideas draw up a chart like this in your English book and use it to plan out your essay.

My chosen topic:		
Introduction		
	Statement	**Explanation**	**Example**
1			
2			
3			
Conclusion		

By completing this chart you can organise your ideas, so when it comes to writing your essay, your ideas are already planned out and this makes it easier to write.

Useful words and sentence starters

To introduce a new point:		To introduce a different point of view	
Firstly … Secondly …		However, …	
Furthermore …		On the other hand …	
I believe that …		Yet …	
Another reason for …		Although …	
To link ideas		**To encourage someone to agree with you**	
Another reason for …		It is evident that …	
As a consequence …		… especially	
In addition to this …		Most people should agree that …	
		Significantly …	
To add an example or idea			
For example …		More importantly …	
A clear example of this is …		This shows us …	
… for instance …		One reason why …	
To illustrate this …		… such as …	
To finish or sum up			
To conclude …		In conclusion …	
To summarise …		In summary …	
Finally …		In brief …	
Last but not least …			

Assessment A: write a persuasive transactional essay

Your assessment task is to write a formal essay about one of the following topics.

- Your **purpose** is to persuade your audience of your point of view.
- Your **audience** is the general public, other teenagers, your teacher and other adults.

Topics

Read through the following topics and choose one that interests you. You can choose to agree or disagree.

- Teenagers have too many pressures.
- Cellphones should be banned from all schools.
- Tattoos should be banned.
- Money is the most important thing.
- The drinking age should be raised.
- Graffiti is a problem in our society.
- We should celebrate our multicultural society.
- The media has too much influence in our lives.

If you have a topic of your own in mind, discuss this with your teacher and get his / her permission before you start planning your essay.

News report writing

Your second piece of transactional writing will be an informative news report.

The introduction

The introduction for a news report is very different from the one we use for an essay.

An essay introduction introduces us to key points which will be discussed further on. However, the introduction in a report usually follows a different format.

What does the introduction of a news report have to do?

- Give us the most important information straight away.
- Must answer the **five Ws** (what, where, why, when, who) and **one H** (how).
- By giving us the key information the writer is trying to encourage our interest in the report so we will keep reading.

A news report provides the most important information first, then the second most important through to the least important in the final paragraph. Why?

When a journalist writes a news report it goes to the newspaper or magazine to be edited. The more important the article is, the more space there will be for it. However, if the report is less important, or if there is a news-breaking story, the report will be cut. Editors frequently cut articles to 'fit' on the page. So by providing the key information first, the writer still gets his / her message across even if a few paragraphs are cut off the end.

The other reason is that few people ever read the entire newspaper. Usually people read the first paragraph of news reports, which is why the paragraph needs to answer the five Ws and one H.

Task: Think back to some of the newspaper reports you have read recently. Which ones attracted your attention? How? Why?

Task: Write the introduction for a news report about the following information.
When? – Yesterday, at three o'clock in the afternoon
Who? – A man in a ski mask
What? – Vandalism of the front of a shop
Where? – Outside the Cinema complex on Main Street
Why? – unknown

Style

While transactional writing is always formal and polite, informative news reports have some extra style features.

Writing a news report

It must:

- be written in the past tense (the event you're writing about has already happened) and you are reporting it.
- be written from an outsider's point of view, not using 'I'.

It should:

- include facts and opinions. However, when using opinions, you must be able to quote the opinions of others, rather than expressing your own opinion.
- include comments made by other people. These need to be put in quotation marks so the reader can see who made the comment.

Keep the paragraphs and sentences short so the information is clear and easy to read.

How do I record people's comments?

There are two ways you can record comments people have made.

Direct speech

- Recording people's comments is called direct speech. When you are quoting a person you must use quotation marks.
  Example: Dana Carter, the manager of this complex said, 'There's just no more we can do at this stage,' when asked about the change to admission fees.
- Make sure you use the person's name and, when necessary, how they are related to the topic of the article.
  Example: Topic: A netball match – a comment might be made by the captain of the winning team.

Reported speech

- Reported speech is generally when you take what someone has said and put it in your own words. Since it isn't in the speaker's own words we don't use quotation marks.
  Example: Dana Carter, the Manager of this complex said that there was nothing they could do about the predicament right now.
- It is best to use reported speech when you want to change the order of what someone has said, or the words they have used.

Task: Change the following direct speech statements into reported speech.
1 'I'm really proud of the effort the girls made,' Constance Brighton, the head coach said after their miraculous win.
2 'It all happened so fast, I didn't know what to do,' one of the witnesses admitted.

Planning your news report

Once you've decided on your topic and brainstormed your ideas draw up a chart like this in your English book and plan out your news report.

Introduction What? Who? When? Where? Why?	

Supporting paragraphs		
Paragraph 2	Paragraph 3	Paragraph 4

Additional information		
Paragraph 5	Paragraph 6	Paragraph 7

Assessment B: write an informative news report

Your assessment task is to write a transactional report about one of the following topics.

- Your **purpose** is to inform your audience of a recent event.
  Example: to inform your audience about the opening night of your school's production.
- Your **audience** is other teenagers and your teacher.

Topic

A recent event you have witnessed or experienced. Some suggestions are:

- a sports match
- a performance
- a play
- a visit from a speaker.

If you have a topic of your own in mind, discuss this with your teacher and get his / her permission before you start planning your essay.

UNIT 8 Poetic writing

Unit Standard 8813: what is it all about?

For this unit standard you will be producing two pieces of poetic writing.
Poetic writing can also be called creative writing.

Finding out what we already know

- Poetic writing is …
- Poetic writing is not …

Task: Read the following sentences and decide which sentences
are poetic and which are transactional. Write **P** (for poetic) or **T** (for
transactional) in your English book.

1. We need to ensure that our future generations are provided for.
2. The warmth of the sun radiated through the pores of my arms.
3. 'Hey wait up,' I yelled at Hemi, but he'd already walked out the door.
4. I believe that we need to stand up against these bullies.
5. Our school was established in 1985 and our local Member of
   Parliament even attended the ceremony.
6. As the storm worsened, the waves began to froth as they crashed
   into the cliff face.

 How will I be assessed?

The two pieces of poetic writing you will need to produce for this unit standard will
be assessed by the following elements and performance criteria.

English written language
Elements and performance criteria for Unit Standard 8813
Produce poetic written text in simple forms.

Element 1
Produce poetic written text in simple forms.

Range: at least two pieces from any of the following categories: poetry, prose, drama

Performance criteria
1.1   Writing expresses idea(s), thought(s), feeling(s), or sensory qualities.
1.2   Conventions of chosen form are observed and appropriate to purpose.
       Range: conventions could include text organisation, use of sentences, paragraphs, use of language features, literacy devices;
       – observing conventions may include deliberately subverting them.
1.3   Writing conveys a personal voice or distinctive style.
1.4   Final product is crafted to publication standard.
       Range: publication standard means that technical accuracy in spelling, punctuation, and syntax is sufficient so that the writing could be published in a class or school newspaper or magazine with a few minor alterations.

Getting started

Poetic writing

Two pieces of poetic writing are required for this unit standard.
- The first will be a description of a person or place and the format will be prose writing.
- The second will be a short scene of dialogue and the format will be a drama script.

What are 'poetic written texts in simple form'?

They are pieces of poetic writing that meet a particular purpose. Poetic writing can also be called creative or descriptive writing. Poetic language is the type of language you use to describe. The reader of poetic writing should be able to see what you're describing in their mind.
    The three types of poetic writing you need to be aware of are:

☐ Poetry

The purpose of this type of writing varies. It can inspire, entertain or describe. Poems can follow any format and they always include language features.
    Some examples of poetry are poems, ballads, songs …

☐ Prose

The purpose of this type of writing also varies. Depending on the format, prose writing can describe, shock, thrill or entertain.
    Some examples of prose are novels, short stories, diaries …

☐ Drama

The purpose of this type of writing also varies. Drama scripts generally follow a particular format.
    A drama transcript usually has lines of dialogue and stage directions.
    Some examples of drama are the transcripts for plays, films and TV programmes.

Prose writing: writing creatively

Writing creatively is a skill you've been using since primary school, e.g. 'Write about your holidays'. The key to developing this skill is to use details to create word pictures.

When you've read a story or a poem and you can see it happening in your mind, then this piece of creative writing is a success. Your ability to picture something or someone in your mind from reading words on a page is what creative writing is targeted at.

How can you create word pictures?

- by using your imagination
- writing from your own experience
- developing your ideas by being descriptive
- creating atmosphere
- developing a narrative voice
- capturing the senses.

Using your imagination

The thoughts, ideas and images in your head help make up your imagination. By using your imagination, you can add your own feelings, ideas and opinions to your poetic writing.

You can make everyday activities seem exciting by using your imagination.

Task: Think of some of these everyday objects and decide on three to four words to make them sound more exciting. The first one has been done for you.

  1   a pair of sneakers – powerful, sporty, smelly, energetic, snazzy
  2   a classroom chair
  3   a watch
  4   a pen

Poetic writing doesn't always have to be about people and what they do, it can be about objects or animals that have adventures.

When animals and objects are given the ability to talk, move and do the things we, as people, do this is called **personification**. By giving an object or animal the abilities that humans have we are personifying it. If you talk about a tree waving at you, or a dog laughing, you are using personification.

Task: Choose one of these objects from the previous activity (a pair of sneakers, a classroom chair, a watch or a pen) and bring it to life. You can do this by personifying it. Write two to three exciting sentences about your object.

  1   A pair of sneakers – *grimy, dirty, snazzy* …
      I kicked my dirty sneakers into the corner and turned around. Suddenly, I felt something smack my right leg. I couldn't believe it! My sneakers had taken on a life of their own. They'd lost their dirty grey colour and looked energetic and quite threatening as they quietly started to crawl away …
  2   Your choice …

Task: Think of a person you know: this could be yourself or it may be a friend. In your head, you should be able to see a picture of him or her. Now brainstorm all the possible things they could do. Don't be afraid to write down all your ideas, even the unusual ones.

Writing from your own experience

Most authors and poets write from their own past experiences. Some write about adventures they have been on while others take past events and then twist them or look at them from a different point of view.

Task: Think about an exciting event in your life. Copy out and complete this chart about your experience.

Event :		
What happened	**Who was involved**	**How you felt and reacted.**
Why? When? Where?	Describe each person or animal involved, explain how they are involved.	Include at least four strong adjectives (describing words).

Once you've completed your chart use the ideas and write a paragraph about the event.

Developing your ideas by being descriptive

Once you have an idea, you can develop this by writing descriptively. The key to describing something is to remember that the person reading your writing only has your words to refer to, while you have the ideas and pictures in your mind already. Your words need to help the reader create word pictures in their own mind.

Avoid using boring words like 'good' and 'nice'. They don't help describe things. Be more specific.

Task: Find six synonyms (similar words) you could use instead of the following over-used and unexciting words.
1   fine – *sunny, bright, luminous, sun-lit, intense, dazzling*
2   good
3   nice
4   bad
5   formal

Adjectives and adverbs can be used to describe words

* **Adjectives** are describing words that describe nouns.
  Example: the *green* desk, the *hungry* teenager.
* **Adverbs** are describing words that describe verbs.
  Example: he walked *slowly*, he ran *quickly*.

Using adverbs can help add extra details to your verbs. This can be useful but avoid using these too often because they can make your writing too wordy, not all verbs need an extra description.

Making comparisons can also help you create word pictures

There are two types of comparisons – similes and metaphors.
See Unit 4, page 34.

Creating atmosphere

The way we use description can help create the mood or atmosphere of a piece of writing. The atmosphere is the feeling behind something. Sometimes we call it a mood.
Examples:
To create a scary atmosphere:
'Through the eerie darkness I could see a glowing light. I felt the fear running up my spine, I tried to hold my breath to stifle the rising terror in my stomach but my mouth opened as I prepared to scream.'
To create an upbeat and positive atmosphere this sentence can be changed around:
'I was curious about the dark passage but I could see a bright light shining through. As my friends all jumped out and yelled, 'Surprise', I caught my breath and a smile spread across my face.'

Task: Take the following sentences and add descriptions to create the following atmosphere. **Sentence:** 'The cat ran in the house and surprised us.'
1 a sad atmosphere
2 an angry atmosphere
3 a happy atmosphere

Task: Write a descriptive paragraph about a person you know well. Think about how you can use details to describe this person. Focus on using some adjectives, adverbs and comparisons. Before you begin, brainstorm all your ideas.

Developing a narrative voice

A narrator is a storyteller. A narrative voice is another name for the 'I' in the story. The narrative voice is shown through a writer's attitude, point of view and choice of words.

A thriller will keep you in suspense, so the narrative voice here is suspenseful. **Example:** The elevator doors opened up to a scene of horror … I stepped back and then pulled my brother back, covering his eyes as if that could erase the monstrosity from his mind. As I pulled him away, I tried not to look but something made my head turn back again.

One way to see if a text you have read develops a narrative voice is to ask yourself:

- Do I feel connected to what's happening in the text?
- Does it make sense?
- Can I picture what is happening in my mind?

Point of view

Everyone has a point of view; it is often their own 'side of the story'. If five people witness an accident or event, each of them will probably have a slightly different point of view. Each person's point of view will depend on their own experience, where they were and what they believe.

First person point of view

When writing creatively the most common point of view, or perspective, is called the **first person**. We read about what has happened first hand in a story from this point of view.

Your piece of poetic writing will be written from the first person point of view. The first person point of view is when the writer takes on the persona of the narrator, the 'I' in the story.
Example: I stepped off the bus and felt a sense of relief, I hadn't missed my stop after all.

Second person point of view

The **second person** point of view is less common and not used very often.
Example: You were born on a Tuesday, you were already five days late when you arrived.

This should be avoided as it can be difficult to use and is rarely used by most writers.

Third person point of view

Another point of view is from an outsider. When a narrator is describing what is happening without being personally involved, it's as if s/he is looking over the characters' shoulders to tell us the story. This is the third person point of view. It focuses on what is happening rather than on the writer's point of view.
Example: 'Little did they know that this would be the last dinner they would all have together. Had Brian known this, he would have spent more time listening to his friends. He would've told them what they meant to him.'

Capturing our senses

Part of writing poetically is to help people create word pictures in their minds. We can do this by helping the reader engage a variety of senses. While we rely heavily on our sight we need to take a step back and think about how our other senses are involved. By invoking other senses we can write more effective descriptions.
Example: If you were describing a garden after a rainstorm you could describe the **smell**, the **feel** of the plants, any **sounds** you can hear, the **taste** of the rain.

Task: Re-read your paragraph about an event. What senses have you relied on the most? If you were to rewrite this paragraph, what senses could you describe? Now rewrite your paragraph to make it more effective.

One way we can become more aware of our senses is to identify common smells, tastes and sounds.

Task: Copy out then complete the following chart.

Object:	Appearance: What does it look like?	Sound: What does it sound like?	Touch: What does it feel like?	Smell: What does it smell like?
Chocolate				
Violin				
Sand				
Your choice				
Your choice				

Assessment A: write a poetic prose description

Your assessment task is to write a formal essay about one of the following topics.

- Your **purpose** is to describe a person or place.
  Example: To describe a person you know well.
- Your **audience** is your teacher and other teenagers.

Topic

Some suggestions are:

A description of a place you know
  Example: down by the beach
A description of an event
  Example: a party or a holiday
A description of a person
  Example: your grandmother.

> **Note**
> Poetic prose writing doesn't follow a strict format like transactional writing. However, you need to make sure that you use paragraphs and develop your ideas so your writing is clear and easy to read.
>
> If you have a topic of your own in mind, discuss this with your teacher and get his / her permission before you start planning your poetic writing.

Narrative writing: developing a drama script

Drama scripts are used to script the entertainment we enjoy everyday. A drama script is a list of instructions and sentences for the actors and behind-the-scenes people to follow.

- Before a performance even makes it to the stage, it is carefully scripted by the writers.
- Drama scripts are used to give actors directions and to tell them what to say.
- Drama scripts are used in TV programmes, movies, plays and even some computer games.

What does a drama script look like?

Scene one

(Night time in a dark and spooky graveyard, with a large oak tree in the background)
Ben   Pssst! Are you there?
(silence)
Ben   Pssst! Are you there Tama?
(more silence, followed by footsteps)
(Tama slowly walks up behind Ben)
Ben   (gets a fright, shows this with a frightened look) Tama, you almost scared the living daylights out of me! Where have you been hiding?
Tama   I was behind that tree … (gestures to a large oak tree) You should've seen yourself! (laughs)
Ben   (looks grumpy)

Dialogue

This is a conversation. Any words spoken are called dialogue.

- For each character who speaks you need to write his/her name on the left hand side of the page. Leave a tab space (two fingers) then write their lines: this is their dialogue.

- Don't use speech marks! The words that are spoken in a drama script come straight after the name of the character who speaks them.

Stage directions

These are instructions about movement, about what's happening behind the dialogue.

- Stage directions need to stand out from the dialogue; this is done by writing them in *italics* or using brackets.
- Setting the scene is an important way of introducing the setting. It often gives meaning to a scene or the dialogue used.

Task: Re-read the example of a drama script on page 72. How does the place and time help support the dialogue (the spoken words)?

Stage directions can also help to add expression to what is being said. This is helpful for the actors speaking and the audience who are viewing the performance.

Task: Look closely at the following statements. For each statement think of a setting that would help support the dialogue.

  1 **Rebecca** I'm so frustrated. I've worked so hard and I still don't understand this.

  2 **Derek**   Look at the tigers. The one on the left looks really fierce.

     Emma   Boring! I've seen tigers before. When can we go home?

Assessment B: write a poetic drama script

Your assessment task is to write a formal essay about one of the following topics.

- Your **purpose** is to entertain/inform/persuade …
  Example: To entertain an audience
- Your **audience** is the general public, other teenagers, your teacher and other adults.

Topic

Some suggestions are:

A dialogue between two people who have just reunited or met.
    Example: friends who haven't seen each other for several months.
A dialogue between two people who know each other well.
    Example: one friend returns from a holiday and is welcomed back home.
A dialogue between two or more people about an exciting event or experience.
    Example: four friends talking about a big party.

Note:
Follow the format of a drama script.
- List the characters' names on the far left side before their dialogue.
- Write the stage directions in brackets or italics.

If you have a topic of your own in mind, discuss this with your teacher and get his / her permission before you start planning your poetic writing.

UNIT 9 Listening skills

Unit Standard 8817: what is it all about?

For this unit standard you will need to listen and interact in a one-on-one conversation and a discussion.

Finding out what we already know

- What does 'to listen' mean?
- What are some synonyms (similar words) for listening?
- What do good listeners do?
- How is listening different from hearing?

How will I be assessed?

This unit standard is worth two credits.

Your listening will be assessed in two situations – a one-on-one conversation and a discussion – by the following elements and performance criteria. Both listening activities need to meet the performance criteria to pass this unit.

English oral language

Elements and performance criteria for Unit Standard 8817

Listen attentively during and interact in discussion.

Element 1

Listen attentively during discussion.

Range: includes a one-to-one situation and a group situation.

Performance criteria

1.1 Attentive listening is demonstrated by focusing on the speaker(s) and acknowledging the contribution of the speaker(s).

Range: indications of attentive listening may include – eye contact, reference to points made, appropriate interjections or questions; acknowledgement may include verbal acknowledgement (for example, follow-up questions, feedback, agreement or disagreement), or use of body language (for example, nodding or shaking the head, leaning towards the speaker).

Element 2

Interact in discussion.

Range: includes a one-to-one situation and a group discussion.

2.1   Responses are clear and coherent.

2.2   Active involvement is demonstrated by using constructive questions, answering questions, and inviting opinions and contributions of others.

A/N.A

Getting started

- *'Listen attentively'* means to listen carefully to what someone is saying. When you listen attentively you focus on what the person is saying.
- … *'acknowledging the contribution of the speaker(s)'* (1.1)

  Acknowledge means to *recognise* and *accept* something. You can acknowledge what a speaker is saying by asking questions, making comments and encouraging them to keep speaking.
- A *'one-on-one situation'* is when there are two people speaking and listening to each other, for example at a job interview.
- A *'group situation'* is when there are more than two people speaking and listening to each other.
- *'Responses are clear and coherent'* (2.1) – When you respond to what someone has said you need to speak clearly and logically. This means that you are *coherent* – easily understood.

Why listening is important

Listening is a form of communication. When we listen to someone we are absorbing what they are telling us and showing them that we are interested.

There are two main aspects of listening:

- Listening to the words that someone is actually speaking to us. This is called **verbal communication**.
- Paying attention to someone's body language – what they are doing with their body and face – the things that aren't spoken. This is called **non-verbal communication**.

Task: Your teacher will provide you with a listening self-analysis: Me, as the listener.

Verbal communication

Being an effective speaker

When you are speaking or listening, it is important that the communication is clear and easy to understand.

To make sure you are speaking clearly you need to pay attention to the following.

Your volume

When you speak, it needs to suit your situation. If you are having a one-on-one conversation then you need to speak clearly enough for the person in front of you to hear you easily. If you are speaking to a group of people you need to make sure you speak loudly enough that they can all hear you easily. Don't speak too quietly or you won't be heard, don't speak too loudly because it may seem like you're yelling.

Your speed

Often when people are nervous, they tend to speak too fast. This can make listening difficult for people. However, if you speak too slowly people listening may lose interest in what you're speaking about.

Your tone

This is the mood or feeling of what you're saying. Your tone is shown through the expression you use in your voice. It needs to match what you are saying. If you are talking about a happy event your tone needs to be positive and upbeat. If your tone doesn't match what you're saying then your listener may get confused.

Task: Read through the following statements and then decide on an appropriate tone for each of them.
Some useful tones: *excited, hopeful, sarcastic, worried, sad …*
1   I can't believe it. I've left my wallet at home!
2   My grandfather just passed away.
3   I just love it when you answer back.
4   My sister just had a baby. I'm an aunt!
5   I've bought three tickets for that raffle. I'd really love to take that new car home.

 ## Being an attentive listener

As a listener you can help make a speaker more comfortable and encourage him/her by doing the following things.

Ask open questions

Asking questions lets a speaker know that you are listening and are interested in what they are saying. Open questions are the most effective questions to answer because they can't be answered with yes, no or a short statement.
Example: If someone is talking about their future goals you might ask open questions like: Why do you want to do this? How will you achieve this goal?

Clarify

If you are unsure about what a speaker is saying then ask them to make it clearer – this is called clarifying. One way of doing this is to repeat key ideas and then ask the speaker to clarify them.
Example: So, when you go snowboarding in winter, what exactly do you do?

Give feedback

Let the speaker know that you have listened carefully to what they have said by providing them with feedback. You can do this by agreeing with their viewpoint, disagreeing or expressing your own ideas about the topic they are speaking about.
Example: Wow, snowboarding sounds like a lot of fun. I'd like to try it sometime.
   Any feedback is useful, even if it is just 'aha', 'hmmm' or 'yep'.

Task: With a partner take turns to talk about one of the following topics. When the first speaker is talking, the other person needs to be listening actively. The listener's role is to ask questions, clarify and repeat key ideas.

Once you have done this, swap roles so you each have a turn at speaking and listening.

Possible topics:
- My future goals
- My plans for Christmas
- My family

Non-verbal communication

When we are speaking and listening much of what is being communicated is not actually verbal.

Non-verbal communication refers to our facial expression and body language. What our face and body are doing or showing can communicate messages just as effectively as words.

Using body language

Facial expressions

The look on someone's face usually tells us what they are thinking, or what they think about what is being said.

When you're happy your face usually shows this by smiling. When you're confused you might frown.

Gestures

What you do with your hands and arms can help you communicate.

Some common gestures are giving the thumbs up and using your hands to illustrate what you're saying. Nodding or shaking your head can also let someone know how you're feeling.

Eye contact

When someone is speaking to you, you can show them that you're listening by looking them in the eye.

Note: This, however, is not always culturally appropriate.

The way someone uses body language can give out positive and negative messages.

Task: Draw up two headings in your English book, **Positive body language** and **Negative body language**. Put the following body language behaviours into the appropriate category. To do this, think about whether a positive or negative message is being given to others.

smiling	poor eye contact	leaning away from the speaker
frowning	good eye contact	leaning towards the speaker
arms crossed	thumbs up	hands on hips
nodding	shaking your head	

Extension

What other positive and negative examples of body language can you think of?

Assessment A: one-on-one conversation

Your assessment task is to have a one-on-one conversation with one other person.

- Your **purpose**: to be an attentive listener **and** to be an effective speaker.
- Your **audience**: your partner.

Topics

Some suggestions are:

- An exciting experience you have had, for example a party
- Where you want to be in five years' time
- Your favourite book/TV programme/computer game/film …
- How we could improve our school
- My family and/or friends.

Your teacher will provide you with an assessment sheet to fill out for this one-on-one conversation.

Assessment B: discussion

Your assessment task is to participate in a discussion with at least two other people.

- Your **purpose**: to be an attentive listener **and** to be an effective speaker.
- Your **audience**: the other people in your group discussion.

Topic

Choose from the topics provided for Assessment A. If you have another idea, check with your teacher first.

Your teacher will provide you with an assessment sheet to fill out for this discussion. Both Assessment A and B need to be completed to meet the performance criteria for this assessment.

UNIT 10 Exploring language in transactional texts

Unit Standard 12411: what is it all about?

For this unit standard you will need to analyse and answer questions about two pieces of transactional writing.

Assessments A and B will be given to you at the end of this unit of work.

Finding out what we already know

Read the following statements and decide whether they are **true** or **false**. If you decide that a statement is false, explain why this is.

1 Language features like personification are only used in poetic writing.
2 A transactional written text is a formal piece of writing.
3 A transactional piece of writing is told from a first person point of view.
4 Essays are written in transactional written language.

How will I be assessed?

This unit standard is worth three credits.

You will need to answer questions about two transactional written texts. These questions have been designed to meet the following elements and performance criteria.

English written language
Elements and performance criteria for Unit Standard 12411
Explore language and think critically about transactional written text.

Element 1
Explore language and think critically about transactional written text.

Range: at least two texts chosen from categories such as – biography, report writing, persuasive writing.

Performance criteria
1.1 At least one main idea is identified with reference to at least one relevant section of the text.
1.2 The significance of a main idea is explained with reference to at least one relevant section of the text.

Range: significance relates to social, historical, cultural, physical, political or personal contexts.

1.3   Three examples of language features are identified using appropriate terminology, and each example is described in terms of its effects.
Range: language features could include – figures of speech, sound devices, choice of words, punctuation.

1.4   A technique used to shape the text is identified and explained with reference to at least one relevant section of the text.
Range: technique could include – structure or method of narration.

Getting started

Identifying main ideas

Main ideas are the most important messages in a text. When you explain a main idea you may be asked to explain how it relates to a context.

A **context** means *where something comes from*. To find the context, you need to carefully read the sentences before and after the main idea. When you look at a main idea in context you are looking at it in terms of how it fits in between the other sentences.

Task: Copy out and complete the following chart. Use a dictionary to find out what all these different contexts mean. Once you have found the meaning, write it in your own words, find words in the same word family and some similar words.

Context	My definition	Word family	Similar words
social	Something that relates to society, to the community and the people we live with.	socially society	community, group, collective
historical			
cultural			
physical			
political			
personal			

Exploring language

... 'exploring language' means to *discuss* and *describe* the language used in a text. When we explore the language used in a text we look closely at the way writing is structured (set out), the topic, the purpose, the audience and the language features.

Thinking critically

... 'thinking critically' means to *understand*, *interpret* and *respond to* written texts. When we think critically we are taking a close look at a text, identifying and discussing main ideas and how they relate to different contexts.

Context checklist	
Social	How does it affect us socially? How does it affect society?
Historical	How does it affect us historically? How did it affect history? How did its history affect the production of this text?
Cultural	How does it affect us culturally? How does it affect our culture(s)? How did its culture affect the production of this text?
Physical	How does it affect us physically? How does it affect our bodies?
Political	How does it affect our policies? How does it affect politics (laws, and the government)?
Personal	How does it affect us personally? How does it affect me?

Language features

Language features are used to make writing more interesting and effective. The following language features are commonly used. For this unit you will need to be able to:

- **identify** and **find** these in transactional texts;
- **explain why they are used**; and
- explain their **effects**.

For the following language features refer to:

Unit 4, pages 33–34: **alliteration, emotive language, hyperbole, imperative, personal pronouns, rhetorical questions, repetition, simile, metaphor, statistics**
Unit 5, page 40: **colloquial language**

Here are some more language features which are commonly used in transactional written texts.

Cliche

This is an overused expression, it is usually a saying which has lost its meaning or importance over time because it has been used too much.

What effect do cliches have?

- A cliche is usually used to make the audience feel more included since an audience will usually recognise these over-used expressions.

- Another effect of using a cliche is to create a casual and familiar tone to a piece of writing, to make the reader feel more comfortable.
  Examples: Hot enough for you?; I'm so hungry I could eat a horse.

Connotation

This is the feeling or emotional meaning attached to a word or words. A connotation is the association we have with a particular word in our minds.
Examples:

- When we think of the word 'party' there are positive feelings, positive connotations like fun, laughter, noise and excitement.
- When we think of the word funeral there are negative feelings, negative connotations like death, mourning, sadness and seriousness.

What effect do connotations have?

The effect is to emphasise the feeling or association attached to the word.

Euphemism

This is a polite way of saying something which isn't nice to hear. Euphemisms are used to take the pain or sting away from unpleasant news. A euphemism for 'he died' might be 'he passed away'.
What effect do euphemisms have?

- They make something sad seem less sad than it really is, a euphemism tries to take the hurt out of something.
- A euphemism can also be used to make something negative sound positive.
  Example: Instead of suggesting that someone is 'overweight' or 'fat', you might say 'big boned' or 'cuddly'.
- A euphemism can also be used to make something unimportant seem important.
  Example: By changing someone's title from a 'Gardener' to 'Horticultural Facilitator'.

Listing

This is when lists of things are included in a text. The list might be quite long or it might include only three or four things.
Example: Jason was the ultimate performer; he played the cello, performed in the school production, sang with his band and was part of the debating team.
What effect does listing have?

- Using lists can provide proof or evidence of something. For the example above, the list of Jason's performances helps prove that he is the 'ultimate performer'.
- Listing can also be used to make something sound more important or larger than it really is.
  Example: By changing 'I have to do some housework' to ' I have to clean the bathroom, sweep the kitchen, empty the rubbish bin, vacuum the carpets and clean out the fridge' makes the job of doing the housework seem much larger.

Slang

'Slang' is casual and informal words and expressions. Many slang words are familiar to us but are generally not used in transactional writing unless they are used to create a particular effect, for example G'day, mate, cops, what's up, dude, buzz off …
What effect does slang have?

A writer might use slang to make us feel more comfortable or familiar with the text.

Task: Copy out and match the following language features to their common effects.

Language features			
1 imperative	2 emotive language	3 metaphor	4 simile
5 rhetorical question	6 personal pronoun	7 hyperbole	8 alliteration

Common effects

A The effect of using 'you' and 'your' is to make the audience feel as if the text was written for their eyes only. **Example:** … you know you want to.

B The effect of using 'them' and 'us' is to create two sides. This suggests that we will be included in the 'us' group if we agree with the writer's ideas. **Example:** They don't understand what we need, stick with us …

C These words are used to make us feel a particular emotion or feeling. **Example:** The fun doesn't stop at Felix's Fantastic Fantasy Playland.

D The effect is to get the audience to think about what is being said to emphasise the importance of the writer's ideas. **Example:** Who wants to be homeless?

E The effect of this command is to get our attention. It directly addresses us as the audience, telling us to do something. **Example:** Buy this product now.

F The effect of this comparison is to emphasise the similarities of one thing or person by comparison with another. The comparison is direct and the effect is that a similarity between two things is strongly stated. **Example:** He was a mouse when it came to fighting back.

G This exaggeration is used to draw our attention to the main idea or to make us laugh. **Example:** I've tried a million times!

H The effect of this comparison is to suggest that one thing is similar to another. The effect is that a similarity is suggested. **Example:** The book was as heavy as a concrete slab.

I The effect of repeating the beginning sounds of words close together is to make them more memorable or catchy. **Example:** Caring Cara captures hearts in Christchurch.

Structure

All texts have a particular structure. This is often called a format. Most transactional texts have a certain structure which is developed by the author.

Writers use some of the following techniques to structure (or to shape) their text.

Repetition of important ideas or words

This is usually done to emphasise the most important ideas.

Bookends

The first paragraph and last paragraph act as bookends to keep the whole text together. When this is done the first and last paragraphs have a link – something that connects the beginning to the end.
Example: 'Once upon a time …' and ' … they lived happily ever after' are bookends which have been used in fairytales for hundreds of years. (Note: These bookends are also cliches).

Most important to least important ideas

This is the way most news reports are set out. It is shaped this way so that the reader can get the main idea from reading the first paragraphs.

Chronological sequence

If something is in chronological sequence it is told in the order in which the events actually happened – from the first through to the final event.

Foreshadowing

Foreshadowing is where the writer gives us clues about the future, about what will happen next.
Example: The first paragraph of a text might begin by describing a knife. At the time it seems unimportant. Later on we might be told that this knife was used in an important event.

Flashbacks

Flashbacks are when a writer writes about past events; they flash back to the past, looking back. Often a flashback will be someone remembering or retelling something.

Narration

Narration means story telling. It refers to someone's point of view. When we look closely at narration the first thing we need to do is to ask ourselves: 'Who's telling the story?' The person telling the story is called the narrator.

For more information about different narratives or points of view refer to Unit 8, pages 70 to 71.

Task: Read the following statements carefully and decide what type of narration is being used: first person, second person or third person.
1   I have always wanted to learn Spanish.
2   You don't know anything about this. You weren't there when it happened.
3   I'm not sure what is going on.
4   He hasn't told anyone that he has won yet.
5   The family parked their car and then entered the house.

Biography of Buck Shelford

The following text is a biography from Alan Duff's book *Maori Heroes*.

Quick Facts

Born: 13 December 1957
Grew up: Rotorua
Schools: Western Heights High School, Rotorua
Claim to fame: One of the most loved and respected All Black captains

No All Black grabbed the public imagination quite like Buck Shelford. He wasn't blessed with the incredible skills of Zinzan Brooke. He wasn't the man mountain that Brian Lochore, former All Black captain and number 8, was. Yet whenever he picked up the ball from the base of the scrum, or received it in a pass, the spectators felt an immediate, involuntary thrill. 'Buck's got it!' they gasped, expecting anything, including the impossible. And as often as not he delivered the impossible.

Buck ran through opposition players, he flattened them with a mighty hand fend, he bumped them off him, he smashed them over, he bullocked for metre after metre with several would-be tacklers hanging off him like insects making a nuisance of themselves. And he swatted them away like insects!

Statistics are not what Buck Shelford is about. Like all legendary figures, you just see the man standing there, his achievements not so much numbers as a feeling inside you, of respect and admiration. As a Maori All Black captain, a New Zealand sevens star, and captain, or the NZ Combined Services tour of the UK, he led them all.

Unfair dismissal
He was dropped unfairly from the All Blacks, a victim of politics, selectors and a coach not big enough to confront him with concerns that his form wasn't up to his best.

At rugby grounds all over New Zealand, the placards screamed 'Bring Back Buck!' Zinzan Brooke had taken his place and another mighty player of greatness was on his way, but most of the country wanted 'their' Buck back. For a couple of years after he retired, they still compared Zinny to Buck, with Buck often winning the vote.

Goosebumps
When Buck did the haka before a test it made your spine shiver and goosebumps come up all over you. He brought the Maori back into the haka! He put the man into the traditional challenge, so you knew what you were in for, and God help the opposition!

Buck's hard attitude was central to his success. He was a fitness fanatic, developing his superior fitness as a PT instructor in the Navy, and when most other players had given up after training Buck would want to carry on.

I went to an All Blacks practice session when they were preparing in Christchurch for the 1987 World Cup. They were packing down scrum after scrum against an invited forward pack – and getting a hard time from those young wannabes! Then Buck roared at his forwards words we can't print here and the All Black pack proceeded to tear their opponents apart.

Much respect
Once during a World Cup test against Wales an All Black lock was coming to the sideline for treatment to a nasty head cut when suddenly Buck's voice boomed: 'Murray! Get back here!' Murray Pierce turned

immediately and ran back to join the scrum. To hell with the injury.

There was another game played against a Welsh team in a gale force wind of 100 kph. In the second half even a tap kick by the opposition would have gone two-thirds the length of the field. But Buck was ready, with a captain's decision and a captain's will to see it was carried out.

Letting the other side have the ball could have easily resulted in a try. The All Black captain exhorted his players, he urged them, he grabbed tiring players and gave words of encouragement. He inspired a win against impossible odds.

With North Harbour he has established a growing reputation as a very good coach. It would surprise no-one to see that name one day in the future as All Black coach. We bet they don't lose many games under Buck Shelford.

Practice assessment: biography of Buck Shelford

Read Alan Duff's biography of Buck Shelford from the book *Maori Heroes*.
Answer the following questions in your English book.

1 (1.1) What is the main idea of this text? Who is Buck Shelford and why is he considered a hero? Provide at least one quote to support your answer.
2 (1.2) How is Buck Shelford's career in the All Blacks important historically or culturally? Explain. Provide at least one quote to support your answer.
3 (1.3) Language features

> **Range:**
> **Figures of speech** – hyperbole, simile, metaphor, euphemisms
> **Sound devices** – alliteration
> **Choice of words** – emotive language, imperative, personal pronouns, rhetorical questions, repetition, statistics, colloquial language, slang, cliche, connotations

Identify **three** language features used in this text. Name each language feature, quote an example from the text and explain the effect it has on the text.
4 (1.4) Reread the first paragraph and comment on why the most important information comes first.
5 (1.4) Describe how this text is narrated. What narrative voice is used and why? Quote an example to support your answer.

UNIT 11 Reflecting on personal learning

Unit Standard 8814: what is it all about?

For this unit standard you will need to reflect on the texts you have studied in class, on the learning activities you have experienced and the things you have learned.

You will need to write about your learning experiences for two oral, two visual and two written texts.

Finding out what we already know

Complete these sentences.
- Personal learning is …
- Learning activities are …
- Reflecting on what you have learnt means to …
- Evaluating means to …

How will I be assessed?

This unit standard is worth two credits.

You will need to write personal responses to your learning and reflect on the texts you have studied. You need to write about six texts you've studied in class.

English written language
Elements and performance criteria for Unit Standard 8814

Write regular responses to texts and reflect on personal learning.

Element 1
Write regular responses to oral, written, and visual texts studied in the classroom.

Range: responses to at least two oral texts, two written texts, two visual texts.

Performance criteria

1.1 Regular writing explores the personal implications and significance of classroom texts.

Element 2
Write to reflect on personal learning.

Performance criteria

2.1   Writing evaluates personal learning activities.
      Range: at least three activities
2.2   Writing reflects on what has been learned.
      Range: includes comments on personal learning in at least two different learning activities.

Getting started

This unit standard gives you the opportunity to think about what you have learnt in class. It is your opportunity to express your own opinions about what you've learnt.

You will be asked to write personal responses to what you have learnt throughout the year, your teacher will provide you with a guide to follow.

- **Six** personal responses are required for this unit and they must encompass the following:
  - two oral texts
  - two written texts
  - two visual texts.
- **Three** of these personal responses must evaluate the learning activities you have done in class.
- **Two** of these personal responses must include your own reflections on what you have learnt.

These personal responses need to include details and opinions about:

'the personal implications'
  - **Personal implications** are your personal feelings, ideas and suggestions about the texts you've read in class.

'significance of classroom texts'
  - **Significance** means the importance, so the significance of classroom texts refers to how important they were to you.

'Writing evaluates personal learning activities'
  - **Evaluate** means to assess or judge something. This performance criterion means that you need to look back and assess (or judge) the learning activities you did in class.

'Writing reflects on what has been learned'
  - **Reflect** means to think about what you've learnt, to identify what you've learnt and what you think about this new knowledge.

Writing personal responses

A personal response is where you express your opinions about the text you have read in class and learning activities you have experienced in class.

Prompts to use for Unit Standard 8814

Task: Copy out the following prompts and put them in the category they best fit into.

Categories:

- Personal response
- Evaluating learning activities
- Reflecting on what has been learnt

1   I found this activity difficult because …
2   I think this text was worth reading because …
3   I found out that …
4   I found this activity interesting because …
5   To me this text was inspiring because …
6   I worked well in this group activity which involved …
7   The most important skill I learnt from this unit of work was …
8   The message in this text was significant because …
9   By completing this task I learnt …
10 The part of this text I enjoyed the most was …
11 One interesting thing I discovered was …
12 A learning activity I enjoyed was …

Guidelines for personal response: visual text – Te Mana advertisement

Text title: Te Mana advertisment
Source / Author: *Taiohi* magazine, Spring 2007
Type of text: visual advertisement

Response to text

1   What is the main idea or message in this text?
2   What did you think of this text? Use examples to support your answer.
3   What is the dominant image in this text?

Evaluating learning activities

Some of the activities we did for **Unit 4: Static image (Unit Standard 12417)** were:

- brainstorming in groups
- learning about visual and verbal features by using flashcards or sketches
- analysing the Life or Death advertisement
- creating your own static image
- explaining the features used in your own static image through a written commentary or oral discussion.

Select **one** of these activities. Describe what you did for this activity. Evaluate how well you worked in this situation.

Reflecting on what you have learnt

Think about what you have learnt in this unit of work. Identify and explain two things you have learnt.

Guidelines for personal response: written text – Buck Shelford

Text title: Buck Shelford
Source / Author: *Maori Heroes* by Alan Duff
Type of text: written biography

Response to text

1   What is the main idea or message in this text?
2   What did you think of this text? Use examples to support your answer.
3   Identify two language features you found in this text and explain how they were used.

Evaluating learning activities

Some of the activities we did for **Unit 10: Exploring language in transactional written texts (Unit Standard 12411)** were:

- true or false brainstorming activity
- exploring the different contexts of main ideas
- matching language features with their common effects
- looking at different narrative or structural techniques.

Select **one** of these activities. Describe what you did for this activity. Evaluate how well you worked in this situation.

Reflecting on what you have learnt

Think about what you have learnt in this unit of work. Identify and explain two things you have learnt.

Guidelines for personal response: visual text – NZ Army website

Text title: NZ Army website
Source / Author: www.nzarmy.mil.nz
Type of text: visual website

Response to text

1   What is the main idea or message in this text?
2   Who would this text be useful to?
3   What did you think of this text? Use examples to support your answer.

Evaluating learning activities

Some of the activities we did for **Unit 5: Wide reading (Unit Standard 8810)** were:

- starter activities
- putting different images into their categories: static or moving
- reading and creating prompts
- analysing the Kapow comic strip text
- writing our own viewing logs.

Select **one** of these activities. Describe what you did for this activity. Evaluate how well you worked in this situation.

Reflecting on what you have learnt

Think about what you have learnt in this unit of work. Identify and explain **two** things you have learnt.

Guidelines for Unit Standard 8814 personal response

Title of text studied in class:
Source / Author:
Type of text:

Response to text

1   What is the main idea or message in this text?
2   Who would this text be useful to?
3   What did you think of this text? Use examples to support your answer.

Evaluating learning activities

Some of the activities we did for this unit.
-
-
-
-
-

Select **one** of these activities. Describe what you did for this activity. Evaluate how well you worked in this situation.

Reflecting on what you have learnt

Think about what you have learnt in this unit of work. Identify and explain **two** things you have learnt.

Appendix

Commonly confused words

The following sets of words are often confused in writing. These activities are designed to get you thinking about these words and identifying when and where they are used.

there / their / they're

> **there:** is an adverb which means in a particular place or at a particular point.
>   Example: **There** you are.
> **their:** is an adjective which shows us who owns something.
>   Example: It's **their** dog.
> **they're:** is the contraction of 'they are'.
>   Example: **They're** the winners.

1   You can put your gear over _____.
2   _____ coming to see us on Tuesday.
3   _____ dog followed me home again.
4   Do you think I should move the bookcase over _____?
5   _____ always talking about that.
6   She's hiding over _____.
7   My cousins just called to tell me they'd got a new TV so I'm going over to _____ house.
8   My parents are picking me up from school, but _____ always late.

your / you're

> **your:** is a personal pronoun which shows us who owns something.
>   Example: **Your** shoes are gorgeous.
> **you're:** is the contraction of 'you are'.
>   Example: **You're** the winner.

1   _____ going to come aren't you?
2   _____ car needs to be moved. It's blocked us in the driveway.
3   _____ not going to believe what I've just seen.
4   Where are _____ shoes?
5   _____ going to love the new jacket I just got.
6   I've been really impressed with _____ results.

whether / weather

> **whether:** is a conjunction used when you mention two or more options.
>   Example: It depends on **whether** or not it rains.
> **weather:** the natural atmosphere, like the sun, rain and wind.
>   Example: The **weather** is unpredictable.

1 The _____ was beautiful today.
2 What will the _____ be like tomorrow?
3 Do you know _____ or not you're available on Sunday?
4 Does it really matter _____ it rains?
5 My dad asked _____ you were coming with us.
6 Summer _____ is my favourite.

we're / where / were

> **we're:** is the contraction for 'we are'.
>   Example: **We're** on our way home.
> **where:** is an adverb which asks the location of something.
>   Example: **Where** do you live?
> **were:** is the past tense of 'to be'.
>   Example: **Were** you there?

1 We _____ going to call you, but we forgot.
2 _____ best friends.
3 I will go _____ you go.
4 _____ you planning on coming with us?
5 _____ looking forward to meeting you.
6 I know it's only Tuesday but _____ both looking forward to the long weekend.
7 _____ did you hide my birthday presents?
8 _____ you at school yesterday?

to / too / two

> **to:** a preposition which shows a direction.
>   Example: Where are you going **to**?
> **too:** an adverb which means 'as well' or also.
>   Example: I want to come **too**.
> **two:** a noun, the number two.
>   Example: I have **two** older brothers.

1 Can I come ____?
2 My friend wants to come ____.
3 Have you been ____ the museum recently?
4 There are ____ more months until my birthday.
5 I rode my bike ____ school today.
6 Where do you plan to travel ____?
7 I have ____ sugars in my coffee.

8 Where are you going ____?
9 My sister has ____ budgies.
10 I bought one for you ____.

accept / except

> **accept:** is a verb which means to get or receive something.
> Example: I will **accept** your decision.
> **except:** can be used as a conjunction or a preposition. It means 'everything but'.
> Example: My family all live in Wellington, **except** for my aunt.

1 I will _____ your offer.
2 Everyone was there _____ for you.
3 How can you _____ that verdict?
4 If you _____ this loan you will need to pay me back.
5 You need to _____ responsibility for your actions.
6 I love all sports, _____ for golf.

know / no

> **know:** to recognise or be aware of something,
> Example: Do you **know** my sister?
> **no:** the opposite of yes, used to disagree.
> Example: **No,** I disagree.

1 Do you _____ how to drive?
2 I waited for ages, but _____ one came.
3 _____, I'm not interested.
4 I asked my mum, but she said _____.
5 I _____ how to change a tyre.
6 I _____ what you're looking for.

off / of

> **off:** a preposition, the opposite of on.
> Example: Get your clothes **off** the floor!
> **of:** a preposition which shows how things are related.
> Example: a cup **of** tea.

1 You can drop me ____ over there.
2 I got ____ the bus at the last stop.
3 Would you like a glass ____ juice?
4 I jumped ____ the highest diving board.
5 Some ____ us are going to a party.
6 Can you pay for us? I'm short ____ money right now.

Tenses

Tense is a word we use when we refer to time. When we speak and write we generally use these tenses: **present**, **past** and **future**.

Present tense

This is used for what is happening now, in the **present**.
Examples: I **am** riding a bike.
              I **like** reading.

Past tense

This is used for what has already happened in the **past**.
Examples: I **was** impressed with that performance.
              I **liked** that movie.

Future tense

This is used for what may happen in the **future**.
Examples: I **will** meet you tonight.
              I **am** going to see that movie.

Task: Read the following sentences and identify the tense used for each, past, present or future.
   1   I plan to study hard for my Science exam.
   2   I went to the library yesterday.
   3   I'm watching TV right now.
   4   I am singing in the choir.
   5   We grew our own potatoes and broccoli.
   6   Has anyone seen my schoolbag?
   7   I'm going to play the piano.
   8   My dog had a litter of puppies.
   9   I am going to play the piano.
   10   When I turn fifteen, I will sit my driver's licence test.

Task: The following sentences have been written in the present tense. Rewrite these sentences to change them into the past tense.
   1   I sing in the choir.
   2   I walk my neighbour's dog.
   3   I am riding on a bus.
   4   I deliver a speech to my class.
   5   I'm drinking a glass of orange juice.
   6   I'm eating my lunch.
   7   I move slowly.
   8   I'm playing touch rugby.

Task: The following sentences have been written in the past or future tense. Rewrite these sentences to change them into the present tense.
1   I watched that documentary.
2   I'm going to eat some more apples.
3   The time was six o'clock.
4   She danced wonderfully.
5   I will see some dolphins.
6   He hid from me.
7   I will ring him.
8   I ran really fast.

Subject and verb agreement

A grammatically correct sentence must have a verb and a subject (which is usually a noun).
- **Singular**: one of something.
- **Plural**: more than one.

Examples

The cat sleeps.
- **The cat** is the subject and **sleeps** is the verb.
  - Since there is one cat the verb used needs to be singular.
  - In a sentence with a **singular** subject the verb must be **singular**.

The cats sleep.
- **The cats** are the subject and **sleep** is the verb.
  - Since there is more than one cat, the verb used needs to be plural.
  - In a sentence with a **plural** subject the verb must be **plural**.

Task: Read the following sentences and decide whether they make sense. If the subject and verb agree write 'Correct'. If not, identify the error and then rewrite the sentence.
1   My friends are coming soon.
2   The classroom are large.
3   I has read that book.
4   We are here for you.
5   They comes to my house each Thursday.
6   My dad love Science fiction films.
7   My parents is waiting for me.
8   I am waiting.
9   My friend enjoys watching soccer.
10   The singers sings.

Task: Copy out and complete the following sentences. For each sentence select the verb which agrees with the subject.

1   My parents runs everyday.
2   Andy run regularly.
3   They is coming soon.
4   The artist paint slowly.
5   Emily play the guitar.
6   She often listen to music.
7   Amy and her sisters is visiting tomorrow.
8   She wash the car.
9   Ben sleep in each Saturday.
10   You has forgotten.
11   They was here early.
12   They lives on my street.
13   Fiona go to practice each Wednesday afternoon.
14   Justin work very hard in class.
15   He speak three languages.

Using apostrophes

Apostrophes are used for two reasons:
- **to show contractions**
  Example: don't is the contraction of 'do not'.
- **to show ownership**
  Example: It is Grace's cat.

What happens when the word showing ownership is a plural?
Then the apostrophe comes after the s (**s'**) rather than before the s (**'s**).
Example: The brothers' cars were at the race track.
What happens when the word showing ownership is a plural without a final s?
Then the apostrophe comes before the s (**'s**).
Example: The women's coats were on the floor.

Task: Copy out and correct the following sentences. Each sentence is missing at least one apostrophe.

1   Thomass article was published in a magazine.
2   This is Eddies dog.
3   My bosss house is enormous.
4   I havent been there before.
5   Sams best friend is also my cousin.
6   I didnt know what you meant.
7   My bosses desks are made of kauri.
8   Wheres Jamess work?
9   Amys cat went missing.
10   My aunts waiting for me.
11   They werent prepared for this.
12   Her cousins friends are all coming. (*There could be two answers here.*)
13   She found the beanie she wanted in the mens section of the shop.

Index

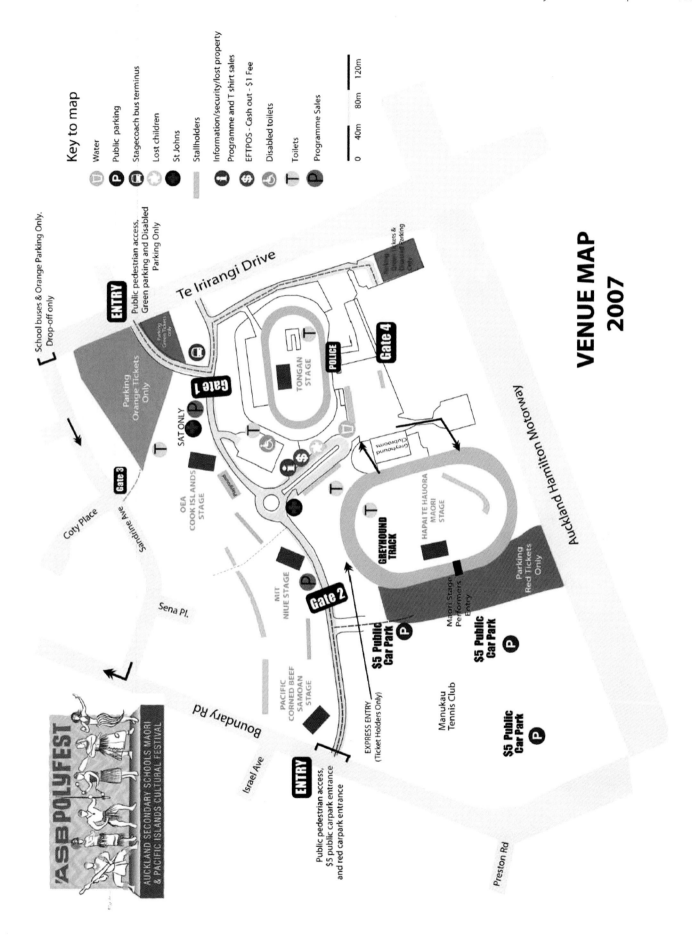

VENUE MAP 2007

Key to map

- Water
- Public parking
- Stagecoach bus terminus
- Lost children
- St Johns
- Stallholders
- Information/security/lost property
- Programme and T shirt sales
- EFTPOS - Cash out - $1 Fee
- Disabled toilets
- Toilets
- Programme Sales

0   40m   80m   120m

ASB POLYFEST
AUCKLAND SECONDARY SCHOOLS MAORI & PACIFIC ISLANDS CULTURAL FESTIVAL

School buses & Orange Parking Only. Drop-off only

ENTRY
Public pedestrian access, Green parking and Disabled Parking Only

Te Irirangi Drive

Parking Green Tickets Only

ENTRY

Parking Orange Tickets Only

Gate 3

Gate 1

SAT ONLY

TONGAN STAGE

POLICE

Gate 4

Parking Green Tickets & Disabled Parking Only

Coty Place

Sardine Ave

OEA COOK ISLANDS STAGE

Greyhound Clubrooms

GREYHOUND TRACK

HAPAI TE HAUORA MAORI STAGE

Auckland Hamilton Motorway

Sena Pl.

MIT NIUE STAGE

Gate 2

Maori Stage Performers Entry

Parking Red Tickets Only

$5 Public Car Park

$5 Public Car Park

Boundary Rd

PACIFIC CORNED BEEF SAMOAN STAGE

EXPRESS ENTRY (Ticket Holders Only)

Manukau Tennis Club

$5 Public Car Park

Israel Ave

ENTRY
Public pedestrian access, $5 public carpark entrance and red carpark entrance

Preston Rd

Ministry of Education. *Taiohi magazine*. Spring 2007

To honour the past **we must prepare for the future.**

Make the most out of school.
Call 0800 80 62 62 or visit www.taiohi.co.nz

This bear should not be here

She is one of thousands of bears held in appalling conditions across Asia for the extraction of their bile. Often locked in cages, bears are prevented from expressing any natural behaviour and can be injured and scarred from rubbing or hitting themselves against the bars in frustration.

The misery starts for some bears with a surgical operation to insert a tube to access the bile in their gall bladder. The pain and distress continues throughout their lives with bile being extracted up to twice a day, often by untrained farm workers with no veterinary experience.

Wound infections, tumours, internal abscesses and other agonising illnesses are widespread.

There is no need for the bear bile industry and the incredibly cruel process for bear bile extraction. Many effective synthetic and herbal alternatives to bear bile are both affordable and widely available. Bear farming is cruel and must end.

For $25 a month join WSPA Animal Rescue and help end the pain for bears and other animals. Or make an urgent donation today. We hope you will help.

☐ Yes, I would like to join WSPA Animal Rescue today with a regular monthly donation of $25.00.   Donations of $2 or more are tax deductible.

OR

☐ I would like to give an urgent donation today for: ☐ $25   ☐ $50   ☐ $100   ☐ $1000   ☐ Other $_____

Title _____ First Name _____ Surname _____

Address _____ Postcode _____

Email _____ Phone _____ Mobile _____

☐ **Please send me a direct debit form**

☐ **Please debit this amount to my credit card** ☐ Visa ☐ MasterCard ☐ Amex ☐ Diners   No. ☐☐☐☐ ☐☐☐☐ ☐☐☐☐ ☐☐☐☐

Signature _____ Expiry _____   ☐ Please tick if you don't want to recieve information from WSPA.

Return coupon to: WSPA Australia, GPO Box 3294, Sydney NSW 2001.

Call 1300 13 9772 or go to www.wspa.org.au/bearbile

WSPA
World Society for the Protection of Animals